PRAISE FOR

10 LEADERSHIP VIRTUES FOR DISRUPTIVE TIMES

"One of the first calls I make during disruptive times is to Tom Ziglar. In addition to being incredibly positive, he's incredibly practical and I always walk away from our time together renewed, refreshed, and recalibrated for success. That's my favorite thing about his new book. It feels like a phone call with a wise, caring friend. Pick up a copy and you'll immediately see what I mean!"

—JON ACUFF, *NEW YORK TIMES* BESTSELLING AUTHOR OF *SOUNDTRACKS: THE SURPRISING SOLUTION TO OVERTHINKING*

"Timeless wisdom for a new era. Once again, Tom Ziglar reminds us of what's truly important."

—SETH GODIN, AUTHOR, *THE PRACTICE*

"Michael Hyatt & Co. has worked remotely for a decade, and Tom Ziglar is exactly right: work-from-home is here to stay. This book is a blueprint for maintaining engagement and productivity through the transition from office to home—or vice versa. I recommend it!"

—MICHAEL HYATT, *WALL STREET JOURNAL* BESTSELLING COAUTHOR OF *THE VISION DRIVEN LEADER*

"If you're not growing, you're dying. In this book, Tom lays out ten transformational virtues to grow your leadership and help you stay relevant in times of change and challenge."

—DAVE RAMSEY, BESTSELLING AUTHOR AND RADIO HOST

"Leadership and legacy must be lived. Current events, uncertainty, along with life experiences are forever changing. Ziglar Inc. and Tom Ziglar have done it again . . . provided a contemporary road map—grounded in timeless virtues—for personal and career success, a road map to live your legacy."

—AARON ALEJANDRO, EXECUTIVE DIRECTOR, TEXAS FFA FOUNDATION

"His father famously wrote a book called *Born to Win!* Today, Zig's son, Tom Ziglar, has authored the book he was born to write. *10 Leadership Virtues for Disruptive Times* contains shocking new solutions to challenges that have plagued the business world for decades. Corporate America has been waiting for this one."

—ANDY ANDREWS, *NEW YORK TIMES* BESTSELLING AUTHOR OF *THE TRAVELER'S GIFT* AND *THE NOTICER*, FOUNDER OF WISDOMHARBOUR.COM

"Coach Leadership is the key to unlocking your team's top performance. This book by Tom Ziglar combines everything that is crucial—the WHO and the HOW to game-changing Coach Leadership."

—BOB BEAUDINE, CEO, AUTHOR, SPEAKER

"Tom Ziglar nailed it with this one—and at the perfect time! He does a masterful job of answering the questions all leaders want to know: What has changed in the workforce? Why has it changed? And, most important, how can I lead my team to great heights through this disruptive new norm? The game has changed forever. Ziglar shows you exactly how to turn today's leadership challenges into fresh opportunities; gives you a bird's-eye view into what your team (employees) are thinking, what attracts and motivates them in these uncertain times, and why this is absolutely the best time in history to be an outstanding Coach Leader."

—BILLY COX, AUTHOR, SPEAKER, AND BUSINESS STRATEGIST

"We have seen what it takes to achieve excellence, and we know that through excellence there are infinite possibilities. Tom Ziglar's book is all about finding excellence in the middle of disruption."

—CASEY CUNNINGHAM, CEO AND FOUNDER, XINNIX

"For such a time as this. *10 Leadership Virtues for Disruptive Times* addresses profoundly these challenging times we have all become far too accustomed to during recent months. This timely book provides practical skills and applications that will develop much needed Coach Leaders. These equipped leaders will, in turn, serve, support, and develop others in their circle of influence during disruptive times."

—M. KEVIN DAVIS, ENTREPRENEUR, SPEAKER, COACH, AND TRAINER

"Tom's objective has always been to improve the lives of those who struggle. For those who are doing well, he has a unique way of bringing out their best and taking them to the next level! His latest masterpiece is an awe-inspiring testament to how he accomplishes and demonstrates his exclusive methodology. He outlines in a concise manner the essential mechanisms necessary to lift people up and become the leaders they were born to be. Good leaders challenge themselves every day, and for people who want to embrace that challenge, this is a must-read book."

—BRYAN DODGE

"Somehow the Ziglar message manages to be both timeless and relevant to a rapidly changing business environment. Don't hesitate to buy this book for every leader you know."

—CHRIS GUILLEBEAU, AUTHOR OF *THE MONEY TREE* AND *THE $100 STARTUP*

"After I finished reading Tom's first book, *Choose to Win*, it transformed me. When he mentioned the release of his new book, I thought to myself, *how could he top it?* He did! I've coached in the sports and business world for more than forty years. I know the winning that happens under the lights on Friday nights is the direct result of the coach's ability to effectively handle chaos Monday through Thursday. *10 Leadership Virtues for Disruptive Times* provides the winning formula for building and maintaining positive relationships that every Coach Leader is looking for. I know this is an old coach's cliché, but it doesn't mean it's not true, this book is a game-changer!"

—DR. NATE HEARNE, PRESIDENT AND FOUNDER,
EULESS LOAVES AND FISHES FOUNDATION

"What a great read and solid information! This is a timely and much-needed manual for smoothly transitioning from the traditional, pre-pandemic office environment to the dynamic new work options made necessary by working from home."

—TOM HOPKINS, AUTHOR OF *HOW TO MASTER THE ART OF SELLING* AND *WHEN BUYERS SAY NO*

"This book is the secret weapon every bold and flexible leader needs in our exponentially changing environment."

—DR. BENJAMIN HARDY, ORGANIZATIONAL PSYCHOLOGIST
AND BESTSELLING COAUTHOR OF *WHO NOT HOW*

"What I enjoyed most about this book is Tom's commitment and consistency to the virtues and values necessary for achieving excellence in leadership."

—DAVID MATTSON, AUTHOR AND CEO, SANDLER TRAINING

"In this age of rapid and relentless change, it's reassuring to recognize that the most important elements of personal and business success have not changed. These ten virtues of great leaders remind us that how we lead ourselves will be reflected in our effectiveness in leading others."

—DAN MILLER, AUTHOR OF 48 DAYS TO THE WORK YOU LOVE, AND HOST OF THE 48 DAYS PODCAST

"With the chaos of today and the overwhelming reach of media, the culture is drowning in confusion and doubt. We've never desired people and sources we can trust more than now. In this book, Tom brings us back to the truth—and the opportunity. He deftly lists what you'll recognize is the 'right thing to do,' exposes that it's also the most profitable, and explains why. For me, it's a root issue when most books on leadership are symptomatic. Don't just read it. Study it and own the wisdom for yourself."

—KEVINMILLER.CO, HONORED CONVERSATIONALIST, 52 MILLION DOWNLOADS AND COUNTING, MOTIVE PODCAST, TRUE LIFE PODCAST, AND THE ZIGLAR SHOW

"Fact: either disruption drives change, or change can lead to disruption. This powerful book by Tom Ziglar shares how we leverage the wave of disruption to have the greatest impact as we change."

—MICHAEL NORTON, CEO AND FOUNDER, TRAMAZING

"When Tom Ziglar speaks, I listen to him. And when he writes, I read his work. Tom has the rare gift of blending beautifully the insights of his father with the wisdom of the ages in a practical manner that elevates the way we lead, live, and impact in our world today. With his most recent book, he offers applicable and transformative insights into not only dealing with the complexities of the world we live in but how effectively embracing them changes not only our personal world, but the world itself. Read this book."

—JOHN O'LEARY, #1 NATIONAL BESTSELLING AUTHOR OF ON FIRE AND HOST OF THE LIVE INSPIRED PODCAST.

"Any leader who utilizes a coaching leadership style will be far more effective than any leader using any other style. And any leader that practices the ten virtues outlined in this book will be much more effective in leading others."

—HOWARD PARTRIDGE, INTERNATIONAL BUSINESS COACH;
ZIGLAR'S EXCLUSIVE SMALL BUSINESS COACH

"Tom Ziglar offers a timely guidebook that will inspire, guide, and teach leaders to up their leadership game. *10 Leadership Virtues for Disruptive Times* teaches leaders how to embrace challenges, manage change, and equip the next generation for explosive growth."

—SKIP PRICHARD, PRESIDENT AND CEO, OCLC, INC.;
WSJ BESTSELLING AUTHOR OF *THE BOOK OF MISTAKES:
9 SECRETS TO CREATING A SUCCESSFUL FUTURE*

"This is a wonderful, thoughtful book, loaded with great ideas and insights that quickly unlock your inner ability to set and achieve business goals. You learn the essential leadership skills you need to release the ability of each person to get more of the essential business results."

—BRIAN TRACY, SPEAKER, AUTHOR, CONSULTANT

"Tom Ziglar hits the bull's-eye with this timely, must-read book. By internalizing and living these ten critical virtues, the authentic Coach Leaders maximize productivity and resilience in their teams by inspiration, rather than intimidation. A powerful lighthouse in a stormy sea of constant change!"

—DENIS WAITLEY, AUTHOR, *THE NEW PSYCHOLOGY OF WINNING*

"What a breath of much-needed fresh air Tom Ziglar brings to the marketplace with his new book. Tom gets to the heart of what authentic leadership is, caring about and communicating with people to get both individual and group results! Transformation is possible when applying the proven principles Tom shares in this book!"

—KYLE WILSON, FOUNDER OF KYLEWILSON.COM AND
JIM ROHN INT.; AUTHOR OF *SUCCESS HABITS OF SUPER ACHIEVERS*

"Tom's new book is the perfect charge we need for business owners right now. We could not have predicted this landscape even three years ago and, as always, the Ziglar Corporation is there, leading us with integrity into this new age of business, relationship, and legacy."

—CARRIE WILKERSON, AUTHOR, SPEAKER, BUSINESS CONSULTANT

"Timely and compelling! Tom Ziglar does a masterful job of communicating the importance of compassionate and purposeful leadership, which is especially relevant at a time when organizational leaders are struggling with reengaging their teams in a post-pandemic environment. Return-to-work issues are ubiquitous now. The onus is on the leader to envision a positive future, which is changing rapidly, and to unleash the performance potential of each individual on the team. *10 Leadership Virtues* will help you do it."

—DR. ELI JONES, ACADEMIC THOUGHT LEADER, AUTHOR, AND SPEAKER

10 Leadership Virtues

for

DISRUPTIVE

Times

Coaching Your Team Through
Immense Change and Challenge

Tom Ziglar

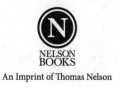

NELSON
BOOKS

An Imprint of Thomas Nelson

10 Leadership Virtues for Disruptive Times

© 2021 Tom Ziglar

Published in Nashville, Tennessee, by Nelson Books, an imprint of Thomas Nelson. Nelson Books and Thomas Nelson are registered trademarks of HarperCollins Christian Publishing, Inc.

Published in association with the literary agency of Literary Management Group, LLC.

Thomas Nelson titles may be purchased in bulk for educational, business, fundraising, or sales promotional use. For information, please e-mail SpecialMarkets@ThomasNelson.com.

ISBN 978-1-4002-0958-3 (audiobook)
ISBN 978-1-4002-0957-6 (eBook)
ISBN 978-1-4002-3213-0 (IE)
ISBN 978-1-4002-0956-9 (HC)

Library of Congress Control Number: 2021945766

Printed in the United States of America
21 22 23 24 25 LSC 10 9 8 7 6 5 4 3 2 1

Contents

CONTENTS

FOREWORD

I'm a raving fan of Tom Ziglar. I'm so pleased that he has kept the family tradition of being a major spokesperson for humanizing leadership—the heart of his new book, *10 Leadership Virtues for Disruptive Times: Coaching Your Team Through Immense Change and Challenge.*

The first two chapters of Tom's book focus on disruptions faced by organizations worldwide due to the pandemic and rapid changes in technology. These disruptions have led to major shifts in human values and priorities. Many folks whose main focus had been work and career are now prioritizing quality of life, including the flexibility of remote work. In fact, a growing number of people are so motivated by work-life balance issues that they resign from their job when they discover their employer doesn't share these values. As a result, leaders in organizations are compelled to rapidly adapt to managing hybrid work teams. The biggest challenge in business today is attracting, engaging, and retaining high performers.

I agree with Tom that the answers to this challenge are found in Tom's concepts of Coach Leadership. A Coach Leader leads, values, and lives out Tom's ten leadership virtues, which are based on my favorite biblical passage, 1 Corinthians 13. These virtues are also the key characteristics of a servant leader.

Chapters 3 through 12 detail each of the ten virtues and how to implement them in your quest to become a Coach Leader. The stories, examples, and self-study questions in each chapter will help you better understand each virtue so you can effectively apply it to your leadership style.

Chapter 13 discusses the concepts of love, vulnerability, and legacy—food for thought that will help you grow into your future as a Coach Leader. And the appendix section includes several valuable tools: detailed steps for becoming a Coach Leader, a coaching conversation worksheet and sample script, and an introduction to the DISC Model.

Read *10 Leadership Virtues for Disruptive Times* and apply its strategies. Being a Coach Leader—and inspiring those you lead to do the same—will make a positive difference in your life and the lives of others at home, at work, and in your community.

Ken Blanchard
Chief spiritual officer of the Ken Blanchard Companies
Coauthor of *The New One Minute Manager*® and
Leading at a Higher Level

CHAPTER 1

EVERYTHING CHANGED

The Disruption Vaccine

The reports had been coming in for several months. China was battling a virus and it was spreading. Italy became a hotbed, and the news reports began escalating. Cases started popping up in the United States. The COVID-19 pandemic was here, and the world went on lockdown. Suddenly everything changed.

Restaurants closed, streets emptied, and office workers were sent home. Hotels, airlines, professional sports leagues, churches, and any type of business that required meeting in person were suddenly at risk and fundamentally changed. Disruption, challenge, and change were here, impacting every area of our lives.

Pivot

Working from home and meeting on Zoom became the new way of life for millions of people. Worry, anxiety, and depression became talking points on the news and in the workplace—wherever that workplace was. Mental health and well-being quickly became the number-one issue of HR executives in large companies. IT executives began to pivot and invest in infrastructure and technology to make it easier for employees to work from home.

Something strange happened: productivity went up for those whose jobs could be done from home. Actual work hours increased because of saved commute times. Flexible schedules replaced rigid work hours. Getting things done became more important than doing things at headquarters.

Work-life balance took on a new meaning. Managing kids in the background while meeting online with clients and answering homework questions at the same time became commonplace. Some companies and people thrived. Others, however, really struggled. Over time, more and more people settled in and adapted to the changes. A January 2021 survey by PWC revealed that more than half of all employees want to work from home at least three days a week.

The disruption of the 2020–2021 COVID-19 pandemic has forever changed the way work will be done. I believe the people who embrace this change will find that opportunities to grow and make a difference have never been better. And there's more coming.

Exhibit A: The Flying Car

In January 2021 Cadillac announced it was developing a flying car with

- artificial intelligence (AI) that replaces the need for a pilot,
- 5G wireless capability with the connection speed to keep the car's AI updated,

- superfast computing that can process millions of bits of information,
- battery technology that is both lightweight and energy efficient, and
- failsafe integration; for example, each engine or rotary blade powered by its own battery.

Exhibit B: Your Virtual Reality (VR) Life

Imagine having a meeting with your team, but instead of logging onto Zoom, you say, "Join team meeting," and suddenly, on your contact lenses, you are in a conference room with your team. The technology is so good, you cannot tell the difference between sitting at the virtual conference table with your team or doing so in person. Quantum computing and AI are making this possible. Quantum computing has already been measured at over 100 *trillion* times faster than regular computing. You can see every expression, every body movement, everything you would see in a face-to-face meeting. You also love the fact you save an hour a day in commuting and can live in a more affordable place with access to hiking trails from your backyard.

The meeting is over, so you shut down and let the car know you will be ready in five minutes to meet with friends for a quick hike on your favorite trail. Like clockwork, the driverless car pulls up to your front door. You shut down your office/gym, which a 3D printer created and built in what was formerly your garage. You don't need a garage anymore, since you don't own cars, because a car subscription costs much less than owning, based on the fact your cars were sitting unused 85 percent of the time.

The hiking spot is ten minutes away, and your wearable device (you might already have an Apple watch) lets you know everyone will be there on time. So you wrap up some emails on the pop-up work-station in the car, which automatically recognizes and gives you access to everything through biometric validation.

The hike and the conversation are fantastic, and you know instantly your calorie burn and recommended exercise routine for when you get back home to make sure all your muscles get the appropriate amount of exercise for the day. As you are finishing your conversation with your friends, you call for the car, which appears two minutes later for the ride home.

On the way home, your wearable device sends you a health notice. Something in your numbers is a little off, and the system suggests a VR appointment with a doctor for a quick consult. You agree, and it is scheduled for twenty minutes later. You get home, get some water, head to your office, and put on the VR headset. Within thirty seconds your doctor comes on, and, based on the data collected from your wearable device, which constantly monitors more than a hundred different body functions, the doctor recommends a couple of tests based on the artificial intelligence review of your data. You agree, because AI and constant monitoring have increased life expectancy and recovery times dramatically over the last few years.

Within an hour the Amazon Prime Health (APH) drone drops off the test kit. You provide the blood and urine samples and then message APH that the samples are in the secure pickup box out front. Five minutes later they are on the way to the lab, and an hour later your personalized prescription, based on your DNA, is headed by drone to your house, as the lab's results have been processed. Once again you are grateful you no longer need to have symptoms in order to know you will be getting a cold or flu in the next twenty-four hours, and you get well before you even feel sick.

Now it's time to get back to work. You have a team to lead! You are grateful as you realize each team member has the same setup and resources as you, and each lives where they want to. You put on the VR headset and enter your virtual office. The office view is amazing! Outside the window is the mountain with all the trails you love to hike. You virtually walk to Lisa's office for a quick conversation about your project. Her office has a remarkable view as well, the South Carolina beach where she grew up.

Quantum computing, VR, 5G, and even augmented reality (AR) reduce costs, save enormous amounts of time, and increase performance.[1]

Sound crazy? It might be a few years away, and it might look different from what's been described here, but you need to know this: you have a choice as to how you embrace it. Those who embrace change are the ones who will create the future, serve their people, and solve problems in the best possible ways.

If any of the following have impacted you, then the future is already here:

- Tens of thousands of businesses and millions of people have discovered they can work from home.
- Millions of people have learned to use Zoom and other technologies to have online meetings and training webinars.
- Home offices by the millions have been created in whatever rooms could be easily converted into makeshift Zoom studios.
- The roller coaster of accelerating change and sudden stops to business as usual has created a remote workforce that is anxious, dazed, isolated, and longing for real connection. Today the term *blended workforce* means a workforce composed of traditional workers who work onsite, workers who work onsite two to three days a week, and full-time remote workers.

What Do We Do Now?

It's not what happens to you that determines how far you
will go in life; it is how you handle what happens to you.

—Zig Ziglar

As we come out of the pandemic and prepare for whatever the
winds of change and challenge may bring, we can be certain about the
following:

- We will learn and grow through the challenges ahead.
- Business will never be done the same way again.
- We will always have a choice: either fold up and go home or
  rise up and create a better world.

Throughout history, each time we have experienced a major socie-
tal shift, we have faced new questions. For example, at the end of World
War I, US government planners detected a potential problem. Millions
of Americans had left their farms and moved to the cities in response
to new opportunities related to the war effort. This relocation of the
population left the country open to devastation caused by potential
famine.

The planners focused on the question, How do we make sure we
have enough food for everyone? The answer was to incentivize farmers
to grow more crops by subsidizing a minimum price. The American
farmer work ethic, combined with technology and science, led to massive increases in crop production.

The government purchased the excess and stored it for reserves.
Soon it became clear that we couldn't store it all, so public policy turned
to other solutions, such as increasing consumption and finding other
uses for the bumper crops. This led to the food pyramid, a change in

the American diet, feeding corn to livestock, developing uses for corn syrup, and using ethanol as a fuel source.

The question of ensuring the availability of food was multiplied by public policies that eventually led to today's obesity crisis. But what if the original question had been, How do we make sure everyone is healthy? The right questions lead to the right answers.

Today, we're facing a similar radical shift in how we ponder leadership. But instead of asking, How do we lead during a time of crisis? let's start with a different question: What is the purpose of leadership?

Once we understand the purpose of leadership and realize disruption is inevitable, we can prepare for it. Instead of being shocked by it, a Coach Leader embraces and thrives on disruption by focusing on what never changes, namely, the ten virtues that fortify a leader.

1. Kindness
2. Selflessness
3. Respect
4. Humility
5. Self-Control
6. Positivity
7. Looking for the Best
8. Being the Light
9. Never Giving Up
10. Standing Firm

Leaders need these unchanging virtues to embrace and maximize the disruptions, challenges, and changes that are not only coming but coming at an increasingly faster pace. These virtues are the foundation for effective game-changing leadership. They're the foundation for leaders who are coaches. They know their responsibility is to encourage, equip, and support individual team members so they can become effective game-changing leaders themselves. Not everyone has the title of leader, but everyone has the ability and the responsibility to lead from whatever role they play on the team.

The Ten Virtues Bridge the Gap

Picture a bridge over a chasm. As a leader, your responsibility is to help build a bridge for your team, one that traverses the gap between the pain they feel about achieving their personal goals and the vision of the business. When disruption comes, it greatly increases the pain, drawing attention away from the vision and widening the gap between the pain and the vision.

When disruption comes, the ten virtues are essential to bridging that gap between pain and vision! How you live out the ten virtues will determine both if and how fast you can bridge the gap and achieve the vision of the organization. The virtues allow you to do the right things in the right ways. If the virtues are lacking, you will, at best, do some of the right things but in the wrong ways. When building a bridge over disruption, you have to use the right materials or the disruption will corrode the bridge and it will last only a short while. The ten virtues, however, are corrosion proof.

The ten virtues are the key to becoming a Coach Leader who sees:

- The future
- The opportunities disguised as problems
- The potential in every person
- Who we need to become to create the future we want
- What needs to be done now

Coach Leaders help the team understand that true performance is the ideal accomplishment of a goal, aspiration, or objective that benefits everyone.

How are *you* leading, motivating, growing, developing, and inspiring your people who work from their many different locations? The existence of your business depends on continuing to improve your leadership skills in a constantly changing environment. How are you going to keep good people excited about working for you and your business in the face of so many tempting opportunities to work for someone else and live where they want? The best way to accomplish this is to learn and activate the power of the ten virtues.

We Create the Future We See

As a Coach Leader, a big part of your role is to help your people see the future. This means painting a vivid picture of where the business is going and how they are an important part of that future. It also means you have a strong relationship with each person and understand their individual goals and dreams and help them to see that future as well. When those you work with see you living out the ten virtues, and they know you are working daily to create a better future for the business and for them, they will help you create the future you have helped them to see.

The Bear in the Woods

Two hikers had just finished a long, tough day of trekking through the wilderness when they returned to camp and took off their boots. Suddenly, a grizzly bear rushed into their camp.

The first hiker said, "Hurry! Run! That bear is going to eat us!"

He looked over at the second hiker and saw he had just finished putting on his second boot.

"What are you doing?! We have to run! That bear is going to eat us!"

The second hiker yelled back, "I don't have to outrun the bear. I just have to outrun you!"

For our purposes, the bear is today's new business reality.

Those who outrun the bear survive and eventually thrive in times of immense changes and challenges. They are also the ones who adjust and adapt to new business realities.

The authoritarian, top-down, hierarchical, well-educated, fixed mindset, positional, "do it because I said so" leader is perfectly prepared for a world that no longer exists.

While the talking heads were yelling at each other on the news and self-proclaimed pontificating experts on social media were trolling and politicians were spreading more and more divisive, nonsensical, self-serving rhetoric, the rest of the world was asking the questions that really mattered:

- Who can I trust?
- How do I support my family?
- What is next?
- What do I do now?
- Am I fulfilling my purpose?
- What if there is a better way to earn a living and live a life of purpose on purpose?

Asking these questions helps to see the golden handcuffs that trap them in a particular position, because the cost of freeing themselves is too high. Leaving would mean losing a big bonus, a high-paying salary, stock in the company, or some other benefit. Over the past few decades, millions of people have gotten very comfortable with their very own handcuffs. With bills to pay, slow-but-steady career advancement, and a false sense of job security, their handcuffs kept them in a not-so-satisfying job with very little connection to their gifts, talents, and true purpose.

Today, the handcuffs are off. The reality of a no-job-security world and the time to think about what really matters have led to a new reality that millions are already embracing. People are looking for leaders who understand the importance of purpose, personal fulfillment, and quality of life as priorities and necessities rather than something to pursue on your own time.

Leadership Question: Do You Believe Quality of Life Equals Quality of Work?

Several groundbreaking trends were ignited by the pandemic. They drew attention to the work-life balance that underlies so many employees' performance, including the following:

- People moving to places that centered around lifestyle rather than company headquarters
- Big companies embracing work from home
- 60 million fewer commuter hours per day
- Large companies significantly reducing their commercial real estate footprint and reimagining where their offices were situated, from high-cost downtowns to the suburbs where people live
- More time with family
- Better green footprint
- Cost savings for remote workers and employers

- A larger worker base and larger employer base to pull from
- Hybrid schedules of working in the office one to three days per week instead of full time

Coach Leaders who focus on the ten virtues recognize and support the quality of life their team needs to produce the quality of work necessary for long-term business success.

This book is about reinventing, out of necessity, the way we lead and develop the heart and soul of our businesses, namely, our people.

This book is about identifying, clarifying, and sharing the purpose of our businesses with our people so they can fulfill their own purposes in life by helping the business achieve its purpose.

This book is about equipping you to unleash not only the leadership potential you have but also the performance potential of each unique individual on your team.

CHAPTER 2

COACH LEADERS CREATE
THE ATMOSPHERE

T. rex managers struggle to lead and go about it in all the wrong
ways. They lead by positional power, because they are clearly the
dinosaur to be feared. Their short arms symbolize that everything
must be looked at closely and nothing happens without their approval.
Trust doesn't exist. If someone doesn't work out, that's okay, because
they will just eat them and find someone else!

If you're reading this book, you are not a T. rex leader, because you
believe in learning and growing. You are a Coach Leader who knows
about I and Me and Us and We.

I and Me or Us and We?

Are you primarily focused on what you want and on developing yourself
so you can fulfill your goals? Is being successful as a leader important to

you because that will ultimately make you happy, fulfilled, respected, wealthy, [fill in the blank]? Such a focus is all about I and Me.

Or are you primarily focused on achieving a purpose bigger than yourself? This could be the accomplishment of the company or a team mission, a cause bigger than yourself. Your leadership purpose could be focused on equipping, supporting, and drawing out the more capable person within each of your team members. Such a focus is all about Us and We.

Now consider the following questions:

- Can you create the perfect leadership blend of the two?
- What if your leadership purpose were to accomplish the mission by equipping, supporting, and drawing out the more capable person inside each of your team members *and* to develop yourself so this becomes your automatic way of thinking, leading, and living?

In other words, you achieve your goals and dreams by helping others to achieve theirs. This is what a Coach Leader does. Coach Leaders develop themselves so they can automatically equip, support, and draw out the more capable person inside each of their team members. Coach Leaders create an atmosphere that allows the team to thrive in both quality of life and quality of work. Coach Leaders, by intentional design and example, cultivate the next group of Coach Leaders, which requires real connection among team members.

Remote Work Thrives Under Coach Leadership

Over the past decade the trend in leading people has been moving away from a traditional manager style to a coach style. There are many reasons for this: remote working has become more common, younger workers respond better to it, and people much prefer being coached to being managed. But the biggest reason is that an effective coach gets better results than an effective manager, even in a traditional office environment. This is why embracing the coach style has all upside and no downside.

In a remote workforce, it is evident that the manager style is severely handicapped, as it does not address the issues a remote team faces day in and day out.

I asked David Wright, our head one-on-one coach at Ziglar Corporation who has been coaching for more than thirty years, to explain the differences between the manager style and the coach style.

He said that managing and coaching, while similar at times, are uniquely different in focus and the way they are approached. Below is a comparison table.

MANAGER	COACH
Seen as a superior	Seen as a guide
Delegates	Co-creates
Tells (one-way communication)	Asks (two-way communication)
Drives	Empowers
Follows the rules	Engagement
Results	Growth

The coach style draws out the more capable person. Remote workers have more freedom in everything they do, and because of this, they must be motivated from the inside out. A good Coach Leader understands this and turns this into a positive.

The coach style also recognizes the truth of this Zig Ziglar quote: "People don't care how much you know until they know how much you care . . . about them."

Leading a remote team effectively means you will have to build deeper relationships based on what is important to your team members.

Atmosphere Comes from the Coach Leader

In the midst of so much disruption, teams and especially remote workers experience emotions and questions such as:

- Uncertainty
- Fear
- Apprehension
- Loneliness
- Disconnect
- Overwhelm
- Shock
- Job insecurity (Will I have a job tomorrow?)
- Loss of identity (Who am I?)

Now let's consider those through what Zig Ziglar calls the *be*, *do*, and *have* filters. They have to *be* the right kind of person and *do* the right things in order to *have* all that life has to offer. The uncertainty of the world right now makes them feel as if their job may disappear. This puts what they *have* in jeopardy! They start down the dark path of can I pay rent? Make my mortgage? Pay for food? Afford health insurance? It's not a pretty sight! This thought process creates an incredibly dark and negative atmosphere that kills performance and often becomes a self-fulfilling prophecy. This identity crisis is a business crisis.

How do you think your people want to feel about their jobs? A Coach Leader who has developed the ten key virtues knows that how people feel about their jobs correlates with how they feel about their leadership. They want to feel:

- Respected
- Heard
- Safe
- Valued
- Connected
- Appreciated
- Loved
- Led
- Included

Coach Leaders realize the importance of the "atmosphere connection," so they focus on knowing what their people want and lead accordingly.

While managers want results and coaches want growth, we can use the *be*, *do*, and *have* lens to understand why Coach Leaders thrive during times of disruption. Obviously, the results are essential to business success, but the key to achieving that success depends on focus. Managers who are focused on results struggle during times of disruption, challenge, and change because massive disruption means that what has gotten results in the past (the *do*) will not get results in the future. Developing skills that no longer matter and tweaking a system that is not relevant only put you further behind and create dissatisfaction within your team, because your focus is on what they are producing rather than on who they are becoming.

Coach Leaders understand that disruption is actually their competitive edge, because their focus is on growth. When things change, and they always do, how can we grow to adjust and take advantage of the change? Coach Leaders understand that growth requires being more than you currently are. The emphasis is on *being* the right person, because then the *have* (results) will come naturally. Disruption mandates that we change the way we *do* things, and to make this change, the focus of leadership has to be on constant growth, so each team member is ready before the current changes mandate the change.

For more than five decades at Ziglar, we have been researching and teaching the eight things in life that everyone wants:

1. Happiness
2. Health
3. Prosperity
4. Security
5. Friends
6. Good family relationships
7. Peace of mind
8. Hope in the future

Now look at these eight things from the perspective of results versus growth in your Coach Leadership role. If success in these things is dependent on your most recent result, then you and your team will be on a constant roller coaster, because not every deal will close, not every project will be perfect, and not every relationship will be tension free—but the market will constantly change.

If your focus, however, is on constant growth and learning, then, even in challenging times, you are still moving toward success. When your number-one desire is to help your people grow so that job success comes more easily and frequently, especially in times of change, then you have taken a huge step toward creating an incredible atmosphere.

How do you build relationships with everyone on your team and between team members, regardless of where they work from, so the right atmosphere is created and their individual strengths are elevated so that performance is maximized?

Read that question again. It's a big question, especially when you have remote team members. In an office environment, you have the benefit of tons of context. Hallway conversations, physical cues, banter, meetings, and so many other things we can no longer take for granted are part of building solid relationships.

Here is the game changer for you as the leader: because of the physical context of an office environment, your people were able, in most cases, to adapt to your unique management style. This in-person context hid the weaknesses of the T. rex manager. In the office environment, being too direct, too authoritarian, too demanding, and a poor communicator were often compensated for by the nonverbal cues readily found in face-to-face interaction and by other team members who interpreted your intentions to others.

In the Zoom world of the remote worker, *you*, the Coach Leader, will have to adapt your style to meet the needs of your team, but only if you want to keep them, keep your job, and keep your business.

Choose the atmosphere you want to create when you meet with your remote team members and that will change their atmosphere!

The Remote First Atmosphere

In the past, remote workers were an afterthought and often overlooked for advancement opportunities within their companies. They were left out in the cold. Not being physically present to develop key relationships or to be a part of impromptu team lunches and after-hours social gatherings severely limited their ability to be effective in the game of office politics. With few companies having more than 5 percent of their workforce working remotely, there was no imperative to make sure company policies and procedures created an equal playing field for the career advancement of remote workers.

Remote workers who are full-time remote or in the office less than half the time need to be invited in. This is done by creating a remote-first atmosphere, starting with the company's policies and procedures and C-suite mindset. Company meetings, recognition, policies, parties, and evaluations should start from the standpoint of serving the needs of remote workers first. If this is done, the traditional office worker will automatically be taken care of. One of the core challenges of the remote workforce is the difficulty in building strong relationships, innovation, creativity, and collaboration. Empathy toward remote workers, followed up with policies and procedures that recognize these inherent challenges, is the biggest and perhaps most important step in maximizing the productivity and cost savings the remote workforce brings to the organization while minimizing the difficulties created by working remotely.

The atmosphere you create for your team is directly tied to the leadership virtues you live out. The atmosphere you create will either limit or unleash the performance your team has. Yes, it really does come down to you. The right atmosphere creates high-performing teams. Here are three goals you can aim for:

1. **Everyone on your team is included.** Make it a practice to have at least one weekly team meeting with everyone in attendance. Don't leave anyone out. Overcommunicate and over-include.

2. **Everyone on your team is heard.** Make it a practice to make sure everyone talks in every meeting. Keep track of who has spoken or contributed to a meeting and draw the silent ones in with engaging questions.

3. **Everyone on your team enjoys a safe atmosphere.** Passionate discussion is great, but you cannot allow anyone to overtalk or talk down to someone else. Respect for everyone is key.[2]

If you have a large team, you need to manage this process by having both all-team meetings when necessary and smaller groups that allow you to dig deeper.

Consider some biblical wisdom: "Don't go to war without wise guidance; there is safety in many counselors" (Prov. 24:6 TLB). When I read this ancient wisdom, I thought, "Wouldn't it be great to be able to call up some wise counselors at any time and get direction, especially in times such as these?" And then I shifted the sequence of the verse. What if, as good leaders, we created an atmosphere of safety and trust with our team, and because of that, they were willing to speak up and give wise guidance? I have heard it said repeatedly that the people doing the work are the ones with the answers, if we would only ask them. Maybe our people aren't offering advice because the atmosphere is not good. Perhaps we are already surrounded with wise counselors and we just need to create an atmosphere where team members feel safe enough to speak.

Many times disruption, challenge, and change in our business life can feel like a battle. If we create an atmosphere where everyone feels included, heard, and safe, then we have created a team of wise counselors ready to share their insights rather than a group of fearful, disengaged individuals.

The Coaching Process

At Ziglar, we train Coach Leaders with an ongoing process focused on the growth of the individual and of the team. It is a process that uncovers and draws out the potential of each team member and empowers them to make choices and take actions that elevate their overall performance. Here is a model Coach Leaders can use with their teams:

1. **Inspire:** Breathe life into the hopes, dreams, and goals of the team members.
2. **Influence:** Guide, form, and shape the mindset and the will by encouraging team members to make daily choices that will create the desired positive change.
3. **Impart:** Grant, give, or confer confidence to the team members so they get up every day and make positive choices.
4. **Introduce:** Bring something new into notice or practice by empowering team members as positive habits replace negative habits and positive transformation is experienced.

What's the power in this process? The process takes the pressure off the individual since the journey is focused on choices and changes that create growth and maximize potential.

As David Wright observed, "Honor the process and the process will honor you!"

As you grow in your coaching skills, you will also need to understand the power of personality. Popular available personality tests include the Myers-Briggs, the Enneagram, and the DISC Personality Profile. At Ziglar Inc., we use the DISC Personality Profile to help us better communicate with those we are working with and coaching. It identifies each person with one of four personality profiles: dominance, influence, steadiness, and conscientiousness. Then it describes how to speak with each in the way that profile likes to be spoken to, using words and language that is far more likely to get traction. How you say what you want to say is as important as what you say!

After being personally trained by Robert Rohm, PhD, in the DISC personality system, I applied it in my personal and business life. This has allowed me to more effectively communicate, especially with others who have a different personality style.

I am a high S in the DISC profile, which means I am relational and steady. In the past, if you asked me where I wanted to go for lunch, I would answer, "Wherever you want to go." This seemed good to me, but that answer will really frustrate people with other styles. For example, a high D style wants an answer, and they want it fast. When I am asked by a high D where I want to eat, I reply, "Take me to a place that has a good burger."

Knowing the personality styles of the people you work with is a game changer, because now you can intentionally communicate with them in ways that have the highest chance of being effective. Deciding where to eat is important, but that is not nearly as important as reaching agreement and commitment from each of your team members on their business goals. When you communicate in a way that serves those you lead, it changes their engagement and follow-through. This is why I believe, as a Coach Leader, having a tool like DISC in your communication toolbox will make a huge difference in your ability to lead and grow your team.[3]

Knowing your team members' personalities helps you guide them toward their goals. I love the story of basketball coach Doc Rivers, who did just that. Rivers is considered one of the best coaches and communicators in the NBA. When he was asked how he was able to motivate players who made more money than he did, he explained that he would talk with each player individually and ask them what their goals were for the season. In the NBA, every player has a detailed contract that lists their pay structure and bonuses that are based on specific goals, such as playing minutes, points per game, rebounds, steals, blocked shots, and so on.

Rivers would go over each player's goals with the individual players. He would let them talk and ask them what it would mean to them if they reached all their personal goals. He would conclude the conversation with a very powerful coaching question: "Is it okay if I hold you accountable to *your* goals?"

This is powerful! Each team member takes ownership of their own goals, and the coach simply holds them accountable to their own goals.

What goals and personal motivations do your team members have? If you don't know, how can you help them?

The Coach Leader Conversation

One of the things I love doing is coaching business executives and owners on how to coach their people. I work with clients from many different industries and, as you can imagine, when the COVID-19 pandemic hit, it was very disruptive for them and their people. Many essential businesses had to quickly adapt their practices and adjust to working in an often tense environment with customers who needed their services but were also concerned with safety and money because of COVID-19. The Coach Leader conversation example in appendix C is a perfect example of how this approach allows you to meet the challenges of your business as well as grow and empower your people. The time to develop these skills is before the disruption and change show up.

Digging into the business needs with different business owners, it became very clear that most were immensely proud of how their teams responded, as well as concerned with how COVID-19 would impact profitability in the future. The challenge of motivating, supporting, and leading a team in times of change and disruption was a huge issue. The way things had been done would not necessarily work in the future. The question I heard from multiple leaders was: How do I let my team know there may be some changes they do not like (because of possible decreased profitability) but keep them fully engaged and excited about working here?

First, in times of disruption you need to understand that your team already knows that they are in uncertain times. As a Coach Leader, recognizing that the team knows the score of the game is very important.

This acknowledgment creates trust, engagement, and participation in the decisions that are made. Recognizing this allows you, as the Coach Leader, to have conversations with your team. You can use the following as a guide to great conversations with your people.

> Coach Leader: I want you to know that I am grateful for and proud of the work everyone is doing as we adapt to the current situation. We are all doing everything possible to meet these challenges. Going forward, we are looking for ways to increase our productivity and to reduce our costs, so that we can continue to grow and serve our customers while we take care of everyone on our team. I would love to hear your ideas and suggestions.

The team will offer suggestions, such as staggering schedules so that some team members start later in the day. This will allow them to meet customer needs in the evening without creating extra overtime hours. This simple change creates better quality of life and more family time for team members and less overhead because of reduced overtime hours.

Next the Coach Leader can start having intentional one-on-one conversations with team members, using some specific coaching questions and following the Coach Leader Worksheet (available in appendix B and at www.ZiglarCoachLeadership.com.

Now let's break down the Coach Leader conversation between the Coach Leader and team members using the chart we looked at earlier.

MANAGER	COACH
Seen as a superior	Seen as a guide
Delegates	Co-creates
Tells (one-way communication)	Asks (two-way communication)
Drives	Empowers
Follow the rules	Engagement
Results	Growth

Throughout the conversation, the Coach Leader takes on the role of *guide*, helping John (example dialogue in appendix C) to uncover and discover what he wants and the plan to get it. This is done through *asking questions*. This process *engages* John because it is his plan, and *empowers* him as he takes control of his own life and career. The Coach Leader is focused on John's *growth*, offering to help him with his goals—both personal and professional—and his ongoing training. Because the Coach Leader is actively helping John through the *co-creation* of the plan, he is maintaining his role as Coach Leader and business owner.

Intentional Coaching Conversations

Having a great coaching conversation with someone on your team as in the example with the Coach Leader and John is very powerful. Coaching conversations are a great foundation upon which to empower and develop your people.

> "You don't build a business, you build people,
> and people build the business."
>
> *—Zig Ziglar*

Intentional coaching conversations should happen on a regular basis. These can occur daily, weekly, or several times a month. They don't need to be as comprehensive as the example, but they do need to focus on questions, two-way communication, growth, and a game plan co-created by your team members.

Coaching Your Team Toward a Balanced Life

For more than five decades Ziglar Inc. has been teaching that the quality of life leads to the quality of work, and this has never been more true than in times of disruption, challenge, and change, because those times expose weaknesses. If an individual is having difficulty in any area of their life, disruption magnifies that area and quickly impacts the other areas in their life. We have been teaching the Ziglar Wheel of Life as a way to understand this.

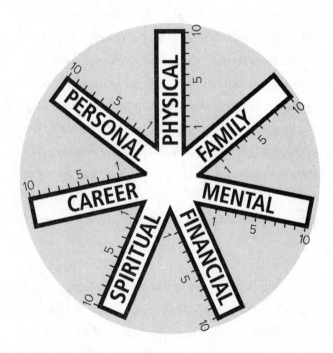

Each of the seven spokes in the wheel represents a specific area of life:

- Career
- Family
- Financial
- Mental
- Personal
- Physical
- Spiritual

You must master some degree of success in each area of life before you can experience the true satisfaction of total success. Every spoke in your Wheel of Life is connected to the other spokes in the wheel. If one or more of the spokes is neglected, the others are diminished. For example, if you focus mostly on career success and neglect family and spiritual growth, you will not be as successful in your professional life as you hope to be. If you make a lot of money and don't take care of your health, you might become a chronically ill wealthy person! But first we need to understand what success is and what it isn't.

As a Coach Leader, ask yourself, Will a person on my team have a better chance of work success if they are achieving success in every spoke on the Wheel of Life? (Yes! Absolutely!) Now ask these follow-up questions:

1. What is the best way for you as a Coach Leader to influence a team member's Wheel of Life? (Answer: You first must have a good relationship with them that is based on trust.)
2. How do you build that relationship with them? (Answer: By demonstrating the ten virtues in all your relationship interactions with them.)

Now think about someone you are leading. Based on what you know about them, how balanced is their Wheel of Life? When you review the description of what success looks like and what it doesn't look like, how successful are they?

Do what Matt did.

Matt McKinley is the owner of Triple M Trailers in Canton, Texas. Several years ago I visited his business, and we discussed how much his business had grown. He was giving me the grand tour and introducing me to many of his people. Then he took me to the main work area, where the majority of his team members have their desks. Matt pointed to a completed Wheel of Life that was displayed in the area.

"Tom, I had everyone on our team do the Wheel of Life assessment," Matt said. "But I did something different. I had them turn those in to me without putting their names on the assessments. This way their information was confidential and I didn't know who was who. I then took all twenty-six assessments and worked up a team average for each spoke on the wheel. What you see here is how we are doing as a team in each of the seven areas of life."

I was impressed and I congratulated him on his tremendous success and on his business growth. But Matt took a long pause and looked me in the eye.

"Tom, I got that right," he said as he pointed toward his team, "when I got this right," and he pointed toward his heart. "I finally figured out, as the leader, if I helped my people achieve balanced success in their personal lives, our business would do just fine."

Yes, quality of life does equal quality of work!

As a leader, Matt understands that disruptive and challenging times are always coming, and he knows the success of his business depends on his people. Matt has created an atmosphere that allows his team to grow, and he has equipped and supported them to reach their professional goals. In the process of doing this, they reach their personal goals even faster.

With the remote-working environment, understanding the power of atmosphere is even more important. As one researcher observed, "Engagement and well-being aren't about the place. They're about the experience."[4]

This is good news for leaders. It doesn't matter where your team is—at home, at the office, or a combination of the two—when you know how to create the right atmosphere and the right experience, your team members will thrive. Creating the right atmosphere requires feedback, purpose, and growth. Coach Leaders understand the quality of life of their people, along with clearly defined and aligned professional and personal purposes, leads to higher performance.

Your success as a Coach Leader comes down to *you*. Not only do you need the belief, mindset, and skills to be an effective Coach Leader, but you also need to exude the virtues that make the right atmosphere possible. The good news is that you already have these virtues inside yourself and you can intentionally develop these virtues so they become who you are. The next chapters will show how to identify and develop the ten leadership virtues for disruptive times.

"Whatever the trend was, good or bad, the pandemic accelerated that trend by 10 years."

—Scott Galloway, post Corona

"You cannot solve a problem until you acknowledge that you have one and accept responsibility for solving it."

—Zig Ziglar

SECTION ONE

WHO DO WE NEED TO BE?

*Virtues Focused on the Character
Qualities of a Leader*

*Love is patient and kind; love does not envy or boast;
it is not arrogant or rude. It does not insist on its
own way; it is not irritable or resentful; it does not
rejoice at wrongdoing, but rejoices with the truth.
Love bears all things, believes all things, hopes all
things, endures all things.*

Love never ends. . . .

*So now faith, hope, and love abide, these three;
but the greatest of these is love.*

—1 CORINTHIANS 13:4–8, 13

What if being an effective leader, especially in disruptive times, really boiled down to loving your people as you lead them?

Do the math and show me the *love*!

Through the years, many surveys have been done about how people view their managers. You have probably heard the adage, "People don't quit their job, they quit their boss." The surveys prove this out:

- More than 50 percent of people who quit their job say it is because of their manager.
- More than 30 percent of people would rather get a new manager than a raise!

And these surveys were done before the massive disruption of 2020–2021.

The ten leadership virtues work best if they're focused on three areas: people, purpose, and performance. Long-term growth success for your business and your people depends on all three of these.

To, For, With

Effective Coach Leadership is not something you do *to* someone or even *for* someone. Being an effective Coach Leader is what you do *with* someone. Coach Leaders are about the *we*. They know that the right *me* starts with *we*.

Early in my career at Ziglar, I was selling books and audio training programs at an event where my dad was speaking. A man came up to me after the event and asked, "I am twenty-six years old and just started my very first sales job. I only have enough money to get one of these two programs, either *Secrets of Closing the Sale* or *How to Stay Motivated*. Which one should I get?"

Dad just happened to be signing books at a nearby table, so I asked him. He said, "Start with *How to Stay Motivated*. It makes no sense to put all the right skills on the wrong person."

This simple bit of wisdom is what the ten leadership virtues for disruptive times is all about. As you develop as an effective Coach Leader, you must recognize that the ten virtues are the rock upon which all your leadership skills rest. You can study all the skills and techniques you want, but if you build them on a weak foundation, your leadership house will crumble when a storm comes. Only when you are rock solid in the ten virtues will specific leadership skills have the game-changing impact you need. Let's get started on the ten virtues!

CHAPTER 3

VIRTUE 1: KINDNESS

Theme: Be gracious and act with sincerity and goodness.

enuine kindness understands that situations and circumstances impact others, and effective Coach Leaders must respond with kindness, even when attacked or treated abruptly. A sincere response recognizes a human being as a person, not a problem or a task.

- Kindness: the quality of being friendly, generous, and considerate
- Kindness is selfless, compassionate, and merciful; its greatest power is revealed in practice to our enemies and among the least of these. Love your neighbor; show kindness to *everyone*.

As leaders we understand we have little control over what others do and say, but no matter what comes up, we can always be kind in our response. This is not always easy, but it's always possible.

The disruption of the 2020–2021 COVID-19 pandemic changed the focus of HR departments around the globe. By mid-2020, the number-one issue facing HR leaders was the mental health and well-being of their employees. Stress, depression, disengagement, worry, isolation, anxiety, and countless other issues suddenly leaped to the top of the list of hurdles frontline and remote workers were dealing with. Kindness is the primary cure for this.

The Three-Step Kindness Coaching Conversation: An Easy Way to Implement Kindness

As a Coach Leader, look at this three-step coaching conversation from the position of kindness.

Step 1: What are your team members thinking, feeling, and doing in regard to the disruption, change, and challenge going on in their lives right now?

Step 2: After you have had coaching conversations with your team members, what do you want them to be thinking, feeling, and doing?

Step 3: How can you demonstrate kindness in your attitude, effort, and skill in Step 1 that will get the result of Step 2?

Q: When should I focus on kindness?
A: Always

Be proactive. Simple questions open the door for kindness.

- How are you doing? (Pause while they answer and then lower your voice just a bit.)
- How are you *really* doing?

- How are you handling the workload?
- Can you tell me more?

Their answers will help you understand what they are thinking, feeling, and doing, and this allows you to respond with kindness. You may not always be able to fix the problem, but you can always be kind.

A simple follow-up note that acknowledges what they are going through, along with a word of support, is huge: "Thank you for sharing X with me today. I know there is a lot on your plate, and I am grateful you are part of the team. Let me know how I can help."

Be responsive. Have you ever had a team member go off on you, another team member, or a circumstance? Don't react! Instead, *respond*. Responding is easier said than done, and because of this, you need a plan.

I have a plan I review regularly that allows me to respond when someone goes off inappropriately on me or my team. It's a simple plan, and it allows me to lead and respond with kindness. I ask myself a powerful question: Would a secure person go off like this?

The answer is no every single time.

The person who is upset and yelling is not secure. Secure people don't go off. This means I am either dealing with an insecure person or a person who is acting insecure because of something going on in their life. Either way, their going off has nothing to do with me.

Once you understand this as a Coach Leader, it puts you in a position to lead in a powerful way. Because the outburst has nothing to do with you, you can remain emotionally unaffected by it and respond with kindness and move to de-escalate the situation. Not being drawn in emotionally is often enough in itself to allow the upset person to come back down.

Remember, when someone goes off, it is not about you, it is about them. They are feeling insecure and something is driving the outburst.

This allows you to step back, and, with kindness, you can discover and focus on the root cause.

Being kind does not mean you are passive. The esteemed medical doctor and theologian Albert Schweitzer noted, "Constant kindness can accomplish much. As the sun makes the ice melt, kindness causes misunderstandings, mistrust, and hostility to evaporate."

As a Coach Leader you are responsible for creating the atmosphere in which your team works. Kindness creates a powerful atmosphere! So when the atmosphere is disrupted, your team needs you to step in with kindness to maintain the atmosphere. The best way to do this is to set the stage in advance. Make it clear to your team that collaboration and getting things done as a team require that everyone on the team is heard, is included, and feels respected and safe. This means that lively conversations are encouraged, but they must be respectful and kind. Establish up-front that it's never okay to attack others on the team.

Here is what I recommend you put in place in case the tone of a meeting takes a bad turn. Let the team know in advance that if you feel the tone is going in the wrong direction, you will step in and put the topic aside, and that it will be reviewed again after a break. Then, take a break or go to the next item on the agenda. After the break you can reframe the conversation to bring it back in a direction that will allow the problem to be solved in the best way possible.

The Kindness Blind Spot and How to Fix It

I had an opportunity to interview leading kindness researcher Shaunti Feldhahn. The following is a slightly edited transcript because I want to give you the context of how important kindness is in the challenge we face as individuals and Coach Leaders in treating others. As you will see, the problem isn't that people don't value kindness. The problem is people act unkindly many times without even realizing it.

Shaunti: The biggest thing that I think everyone needs to be aware of regarding kindness, and we found this in the research with all types of relationships—couples, parent–child, colleague with colleague, leader with subordinate, customer service manager with client, even mothers-in-law—across the board, in every single area, without exception, is that we all have a blind spot. Every single person values kindness, and yet almost everyone acts unkindly.

Everyone agrees that kindness is essential. In general, everybody values it. So the problem comes because, in general, we already think we are kind and we don't truly realize that every day, throughout the day, there are ways that we are absolutely the opposite of that, that we are operating contrary to this value that we all hold.

If you want a nuance, it's not just *be kind*; it's learn the ways you are subconsciously unkind and work on correcting those. Truly, this is the issue. What we ended up doing, as the main research project that the data centered around, is we ended up testing what it is that we can do, either simple or complicated stuff, just what is it that wakes us up to what's actually going on? That wakes us up to the ways that maybe we're not as kind as we thought we were and some of the ways we're unkind and didn't realize it? And what do we want it to be? What wakes us up to that? What actions, what steps can we take that wake us up to the fact that we are acting unkindly? And what actions can we take to retrain us in a different way? And then, once we've built that skill of doing things slightly differently in a way that matters, what is it that builds habits from that?

There's sort of an eye-opening phase, the "Oh, my gosh, I had no idea" phase. There's the, "Okay, I've got to learn new skills here that I didn't realize I needed to learn," and then, "Now I want it to be part of my life so it's just everyday."

We did a ton of testing and ended up settling on this thing we called the "Thirty-Day Kindness Challenge." We tested it in the different environments, workplace and leadership included, and in every single environment, statistically 89 percent of the relationships improved. This is a really, really startling number in social science, because you don't normally see those kinds of numbers.

It's not about being kind, because we already think we are. We have to stop the ways that we're not kind and relearn the good habits that are truly kind.

Tom: I get it. Almost everyone values kindness and even assumes they are kind to other people, and yet almost everyone actually behaves in ways that are unkind. I love your Thirty-Day Kindness Challenge, and you start with just one person (who doesn't know you are doing it with them). How does it work and how does it allow us to create the habits that are automatically kind?

Shaunti: So the Thirty-Day Kindness Challenge consisted of these three items that you do every day for thirty days. And the first thing is you literally don't say anything negative about that person, either to them or about them to somebody else. Nothing negative. If you need to correct your child or you need to correct a subordinate, that's part of the situation, but you can't do it in a negative way. That pattern, and I'll go through what I think are some of the most relevant patterns that tend to come up among leaders in a second.

Basically, you have to withhold all of that, whatever your pattern of negativity is. You have to withhold that for thirty days. The second thing you do every day for thirty days is you always find, you look for and find something you can praise and affirm about this person that you're doing this for. Again, this is just one person.

And then you tell them and you tell somebody else. It's a great habit for a leader to pick up anyway, but paired with not accidentally sabotaging things, it's eye-opening and powerful.

And then third is to do a small act of kindness or generosity for them every day. And that can be across the board. It can literally be, for example, we think of bringing a cup of coffee after a lunch break. That's an act of kindness, it's an act of service. That's one type of act of kindness. But it's just as important to the other person.

I'll give you a common example that everybody has gotten used to this past year, which is suddenly the kids are crying in the background, you're in the middle of an important meeting, you can tell your colleague is embarrassed, and you say, "Don't worry. Go deal with them. It's fine. I've got some coffee here. I've got some notes. Come back in five minutes. We're fine." That's an action of generosity to not make them feel stupid. And to take the extra five minutes, even though you don't have it, there's all sorts of ways that can play out.

Tom: Can you give some examples in a leadership context?

Shaunti: Suppose you are a boss and you're managing a team of six or seven people, and one or two of them, they're great workers, but you get irritated by some of their ways of handling things. Maybe somebody complains a lot. Maybe somebody is always missing their deadlines. But they're really good in other ways, and there's just some frustrations.

You would pick that person, and not tell them you're doing this, to do the Thirty-Day Kindness Challenge *for* them. And you would go through the whole process I just talked about. Identify your pattern of negativity, your pattern of unkindness, and withhold it for thirty days. Look at the things you can praise. Do an act of generosity. Say, "It's fine. Don't worry about the kids. I'll be here in five minutes."

Tom: So just do these three things every day for thirty days: (1) don't say anything negative about them or to them, (2) look for something you can praise and affirm in them and then tell them and tell someone else, and (3) do one act of generosity for them.

Shaunti: By following that process, no matter what the environment is, if you do that, we have found that 89 percent of relationships improved. And from a leadership standpoint, what we heard from leaders, including high-level leaders who were managing an executive team, and then the executive team who are doing the day-to-day management, all the way to somebody who's a peer leader that others look to for guidance, even when they don't have any official authority.

All the way through that change, what every single person found is that, within days, it was that quick, they started to actively appreciate the person who formerly irritated them. They started to actively enjoy working with them in a way they didn't before. There were some exceptions because, you know, a couple of people—I can tell you a story or two if you're interested—they picked somebody who was an extremely difficult personality.

Tom: Yes, tell me one of those stories.

Shaunti: One woman ran a team of analysts and her colleague ran a team of salespeople, and they had to work together in order to get the business development done. So they were siloed, and this structure was, of course, frustrating to everybody. But she had to depend on the work of these people to get her work done in order to funnel the business development process.

Now the guy over the sales department was an extremely difficult personality. Classic New York screamer. And she was a pretty no-nonsense person herself, but this guy mistreated people in his downstream so much that they had constant turnovers; there were just all these issues, and frankly, he was cruel. But he didn't see it that way. He was not kind.

She did the Thirty-Day Kindness Challenge for him because they were peers and her work depended on his people, and his people depended on hers. Within about, I guess, two or three days, the common thing happened. "Wow, I didn't realize I was adding to the problem, because, you know, when I'd be in a meeting, I'd be rolling my eyes a bit. And I'm sure that came across. I was being pushy about certain things that were really his department. It wasn't my place to be pushy, but I felt pretty strongly, and so it came across that I didn't trust him, which I didn't. But I can see how that hurt the relationship."

And so she was committed to work the challenge for the full thirty days. She would withhold all of that and she identified her own pattern of negativity as basically irritation, exasperation, and pointing out mistakes. By the way, those are mine as well. And so she stopped it completely and realized, "Oh, my gosh, this is why some people in my own downstream are frustrated."

You start to understand what's going on after only a few days. About day five or six or seven, something happened, though she didn't tell me what it was. She said, "It was another example of screaming, of mistreatment, of whatever," and she realized, "Okay, withholding my pattern of negativity doesn't mean not confronting something that needs to be confronted. Sometimes the kindest thing you can do is to have boundaries. Sometimes the kindest thing you can do is address things that absolutely need to be addressed."

When she told me about this revelation, I thought, "Wow, that's a great way of thinking about it. I hadn't thought about it."

She said, "It is actively unkind to this man to let him respond in this way to his people, because it is hurting his mental and emotional equilibrium too. So much research has found that you're actually hurting yourself when you're mistreating others. It makes you more unhappy, it makes you more stressed, it makes you more angry, right?"

And she did something she would not have done before. She said, "In the past I would have snapped at him. Told him that he couldn't talk to people that way." But this time, I said, "Frank, listen, I need to talk to you about something important. I know you don't intend to be cruel."

She started with a kind statement, with an assumption of goodwill.

"I know you don't intend to be cruel, but listen, I have to tell you, you are being cruel and it's getting worse. When I started working with you five years ago, I was concerned about the retention rate and people not understanding your management style. But over the last few years we've lost this person and that person and there's a high turnover rate of some of the other people in the department. And we're seeing a loss of customers. Our analysts weren't able to get done what they needed to get done. And I know you don't intend to be cruel, but I think this has gotten to the point where it's impacting my analysts' work and it's impacting the business. I need to tell you that this has to change. And I know you can."

Again, another kind statement, "I know you can."

She told him, "I've seen you handle things in amazing ways."

And she named a couple, which is also something that happens when you do the second step: looking for things to praise every day. You see them more easily now. And so she had the ammunition to say, "I've seen this and this and this," whereas before she wouldn't have been able to say those positive things.

She said, "I've seen this, you've done things this way, it's amazing. But this one thing has to change, and you have to know, Frank, if it doesn't, I'll have no choice but to escalate this up the chain, because it has started to impact people in a way I don't think you realize."

Again, benefit of the doubt, whether or not that is actually valid internally. You might suspect the worst of this person, that they don't care, right? But giving them an out, you know, to save face or whatever, and candidly what we did find in most of our studies is that most of the time the person who's being a jerk, they don't like being a jerk, and they don't think they are, because they can't see it. They just don't get it. Most of the time it's accurate to say, "I know you don't intend to be cruel." That's an accurate statement most of the time.

So anyway, she had that conversation with him, and because it wasn't, "Frank, don't talk to my people that way," she was really surprised when he responded in a much healthier way than she expected. But some of it was she had built up goodwill over the previous, whatever it was, seven days, and he was feeling generous toward her, and she was feeling generous toward him because of all the positive things she had noticed.

She said it was really interesting. It wasn't like he turned into a different personality overnight, because he had years of habits, right? But she could tell that he woke up to what she was saying. And this is one of the principles that we talk about in the kindness challenge. It is in the leadership resources. We talk about breaking down people's walls. We talk about what it is that's causing somebody to have a wall against you. You need to break down that wall.

But we actually found that kindness doesn't actually break down walls. It melts them. It melts a hole through, and the other person lets you in. It's not as if you're tearing down the wall brick by brick. Kindness melts through, and the other person is impacted in a way so that they're the ones who take down the wall. It's a completely different way of thinking about it. You melt through that wall, you touch their heart, and they tear down the wall.

She said that's what she saw in this guy. He never became a perfect manager. He still had years of bad habits. I can't remember how old he was. I think he was in his midfifties. So he still had years of bad habits, but she could see him processing this, and she could see in future meetings how he treated his people better.

He started saying things like "How could you?" and "I'm a little frustrated." He'd catch himself when he'd start the usual harangue, and then he'd back off and say, "I'm a little frustrated because the deadline was here. What happened?"

So she saw a difference. It wasn't perfect, but she saw a difference. That's the kind of story I heard by the hundreds over the course of the research. And it's why the one most important thing I wanted to mention to you is the centrality of not just saying be kind, but figure out where your own shortfalls are in kindness. Identify your blind spots. That's the big picture.

Tom: That was spot on. With all this disruption, such as people working from home, a lot more stress, how important is kindness for a leader in this new world? Because it's not going back to where it was. It's going to continue to move into a new way of working. There's going to be disruption, challenge, and constant change.

Shaunti: Well, to me, kindness, as we talked about earlier, is the overall solution for managing disruption, because what you're acknowledging is the other person's disruption, not just your own. And you're choosing to handle both of those things well. Both your own disruption and their disruption.

One example we found in a previous research project about the workplace dealt with subconscious but very real leadership expectations that are especially common among men who played sports, who saw the goal as being all about the results. They don't care what you do, it's all about the results. But according to our research, that's actually just so much baloney, because we found that real expectations are about two things. One is the results absolutely, but it's also about showing that you're all in with the team, because there is a feeling among leaders that the weight of the world is on their shoulders. They're constantly worried about dropping balls. They're constantly trying to make sure they're going to do well and, by extension, provide for their family. And if they drop any of these things, everything could come crashing down, even though this is very much in the back of their mind, especially among men.

And this ties into our other research about the fact that men look so confident in themselves and women are often surprised to find there's a lot of vulnerability there. Subconsciously, every leader is asking, "Who's sharing the weight of the world with me? Who can I trust?" It's not just about delivering results; it's about showing that you're on the team and that you'll do anything and put aside anything and work late into the night and answer texts at midnight to show others that they're carrying this weight and they're willing to share it.

For many people, it's like the classic pre-pandemic statement, "It shouldn't matter if I have to leave at 5:00 p.m. as long as I'm getting my work done." Well, it shouldn't matter, but it does, because you have the perspective, right or wrong, that the other person doesn't get it or isn't sharing the weight. And this comes from sports and all sorts of other expectations that build up over years and years.

You would never hear an all-star player say, "You know, coach, it doesn't matter. I can catch the pass every time. I'm getting my results done. I don't need to do the two-a-day practices." They would never say that because part of the deal is they're sharing the pain of the team. And they're showing they're all in. It's that same need that many business leaders have, especially male leaders, that have set these expectations on everyone. Now all of that has been disrupted. How do you show that you're all-in with the team, and how do I, as a leader, know you're all-in with the team when it's all over Zoom and I'm not seeing you wandering the halls at 9:00 p.m.?

There's a new paradigm in the workplace, and I think, based on what we've seen thus far in the pandemic situation, that this has led to some healthier expectations. At the top of these expectations is quality of life, because the leaders themselves have enjoyed not having to commute, for example.

And so the question is this, Are some of those expectations returning? Or are we, as leaders, going to say, "I saw how healthy it was when we didn't force people to work in an office and we recognized you could be all-in with a team and still be home with your kids"?

Tom: To me, that's the goal, because what the world is verbalizing is a worry about collaboration, creativity, and innovation by keeping people separated. But I think what you just said is what they're really worried about, How do I know you're all in? Because if I'm meeting with all-in people, it doesn't matter how that meeting's happening.

Shaunti: I know who on my team is all-in. We found out last night that we have to submit a proposal to a partner organization tomorrow that we didn't realize was due tomorrow. This proposal will take a lot of time, and we had already begun, so I texted my staff director at 10:20 last night to say that someone was working on this, but I didn't know what had been done. Since I didn't want to start from scratch, I asked her to send it to me.

Within five minutes she sent me the file because she recognized this was an emergency. So I know she's all-in, and that is an example of a way I know that. Would it have been right for me to expect that sort of quick response at 10:30 p.m.? No. It wouldn't have been, because that would have changed the dynamic from two-sided to one-sided. That's not kind. It's me expecting that from her constantly without my recognizing what is going on in her life and recognizing the disruption goes both ways. This is an example of kindness in action.

Kindness never assumes the other person knows your motive or heart. A true act of kindness is for the benefit of the other person, and the act often changes their view of the situation and how they react to it. Many times, acts of kindness change a life forever.

Following are a few real-life examples of kindness in the workplace.

Frank Stewart is a Ziglar Legacy speaker, and he gave this example:

A quick example of kindness happened on one of my sales teams when a new hire (Curtis) showed up on day one for training without a tie or a jacket, and was about to be sent home by the training manager, and one of the managers on the team who was there to give them the welcome and share about the culture of the organization untied his own tie, took off his jacket, and gave it to Curtis, who then was able to stay, graduated training, went on to become a hardworking, positive contributor, and is still a friend of mine to this day. Largely due to the compassion shared on day one. Numerous others in that training group have told me how that one single act of kindness to a person they did not know demonstrated to them the culture they later were to enjoy on the sales team.

Imagine the scene. It's your first day on the job. What are you feeling? Scared? Nervous? Unsure? You bet! You show up and suddenly realize everyone has a coat and tie but you. You see some managers whispering and looking at you. Dread sets in. You start to tell yourself, "My first impression has been a disaster. They may fire me before the training even starts." And then a manager comes over and gives you his coat and tie. Instantly, a simple, priceless act of kindness that cost nothing means everything.

The manager who saved the day was aware of the mood in the room. Because of this, the opportunity for an act of kindness with a huge impact was possible.

Maybe he remembered what he was feeling on his first day on the job!

Maybe he recalled the Silver Rule: Don't do to others what you wouldn't want done to you.

Maybe he saw the other managers getting ready to follow the policy.

Maybe the manager remembered a kindness that changed the trajectory of his career. Perhaps he had been the victim of an unkindness that he vowed to never let happen to someone else.

Whatever the case, it was an act of kindness, a demonstration of kindness that made the difference.

Joe Dearing is also a Ziglar Legacy speaker, and he related this experience:

> I took a job as a vascular ultrasound tech at the end of 1992 for Bruce Hammond. My wife at the time was pregnant with Tyler, our first son, and she was due in June, so I wasn't at the company for even seven months when Tyler was born. It was a perfect storm. I decided on May 23, which is my birthday, to take eight friends to an outdoor concert festival I had won a bunch of tickets to on the radio. Long story short, I broke my leg playing hacky sack at the Motley Crue concert two weeks before my son was born. Anyway, I put off the broken leg because my son was coming any day. He was born on June 8, 1993. He was purple and he stayed that way for two hours before they realized he needed to be transported to Dallas Children's Hospital ASAP or he wasn't going to make it. On June 9, I had to go to South Dallas for surgery on the broken leg, as it had been over two weeks since it had been broken. Tyler was at Dallas Children's awaiting open-heart surgery, and my wife, Suzi, was at the Grand Prairie hospital. That day, June 9, we were all in different hospitals.
>
> My son made it through, I made it through, we all made it through because, during all this, which was like two months of chaos, I never had to go to work and my boss continued to pay me. This same man introduced me to Jesus Christ, my Lord and Savior. Bruce is an epic leader who continually shows everyone kindness through not only his words but in his actions. Love you, Bruce.

This story was posted on Facebook and Bruce, Joe's leader, responded.

I think you give me too much credit, it was a "do unto others moment." The question is, Does the walk meet the talk? Thank you for your kind words, but it was He, not me.

Kindness: do unto others as you would have them do unto you. It goes without saying that everyone goes through hard times. Kindness can impact a life far beyond anything we can imagine. In Joe's case the impact is rippling through eternity.

George Puia received a powerful act of kindness from a mentor early in his leadership career with the only condition being to pay it forward.

I had just received a promotion to manage my department. I was twenty-seven, and the next youngest employee was forty-two. I went to my mentor, an exec in another division. He met me after work and took me to a men's clothing store. He bought me two suits, shirts, and some conservative ties. I told him I would pay him back, but he wanted no part of it. He said, "That's not how it works, just help someone else." I started the new position looking five to ten years older and with more confidence.

As a Coach Leader, one of your primary responsibilities is to help your people develop into Coach Leaders. George's mentor no doubt understood that kindness is a game changer, and the best way to teach it is to do it.

Tom Zampino is a longtime friend of the Ziglar family and relates this story:

I was working at a small Manhattan law firm. The paralegal who was working directly for me was having a very tough financial time.

The partners as a group decided, however, not to give her a raise in a particular year. The senior founding member of the firm felt her pain immediately. Privately, with me, he pulled out his own checkbook and wrote her a check for a substantial amount and told her to keep his generosity quiet. Very kind, very thoughtful. Very needed.

Kindness done confidentially and with personal cost is perhaps the greatest example of kindness. Years and years later the blessings from Tom's experience are still impacting others.

Michael Norton is a twenty-plus-year friend and a former president of Ziglar. He left Ziglar to work for Sandler Training, and he told this story not long after he joined Sandler:

In October 2010 I faced the darkest day of my life. My wife was diagnosed with stage-four pancreatic cancer. It was bad. I was just seven months into my new position, running a global sales organization, and I knew I needed to take care of my wife and three kids. I was uncertain if I could maintain my commitment to my new employer. Inside I felt as if I needed to resign and just be a full-time husband, dad, and caregiver. When I shared the news and diagnosis with the CEO, David Mattson, I expected he would be understanding and support my decision. Boy, was I wrong.

But wrong in a good way. David not only didn't accept my resignation, but he also told me that he would support me and my family through whatever we were facing. As my job required significant travel, he told me that I could travel as needed and if it was okay to be away for a day or two. If not, I should stay home, and if I could accomplish what I needed to by telephone, that was okay too. He never stopped paying my full salary. The support of the entire organization was truly amazing during this time.

One of the moments of kindness that still stands out as amazing came one day when I was scheduled to deliver a keynote speech in the Netherlands. It had been booked months in advance. My wife and I talked about it, and we agreed that I should honor the commitment and go. I could actually manage the travel and event and only be gone for forty-eight hours. The day before I was scheduled to leave, my wife had a bad reaction to a new chemo regimen they had started. She was too sick for me to leave. I called David and apologized that I was going to have to cancel the trip and the keynote. Without hesitation, David told me to stay home, take care of my wife, and that he would take care of it. Little did I know taking care of it meant that he would clear his calendar, buy a last-minute ticket to Europe, and take the stage in my place.

The thing is this: the event was for a sales kickoff for a client. He wasn't doing this to save a deal or generate more revenue. David did this to fulfill a commitment I had made as a favor for the client. And never once in ten years has he ever brought it up; he never told others what he did or why.

For the duration of my wife's battle, when she passed away, and for our entire relationship, David has always been nothing but kind and supportive. I could share another one of his demonstrations of kindness but will save that for another time.

As you reflect on these examples of kindness in the workplace, take a moment to consider how being kind impacts both the giver and the receiver. Does the atmosphere improve? Does morale go up? What about loyalty? Gratitude? Care? Belonging? Kindness is the bedrock of good working relationships and allows people, teams, and companies to survive the toughest storms. Being kind creates an atmosphere of kindness and allows Coach Leaders to expect kindness from their team. Creativity and innovation flourish in an atmosphere of kindness because there is no risk in sharing new ideas.

Here are a few kindness questions to ponder as a Coach Leader:

- How can you be kind to yourself and set an example for your team to be kind to themselves?
- What questions can you ask your team members that would reveal what is really going on with their thinking and feeling?
- What is your leader struggling with and how can you support him or her with kindness in that struggle?

CHAPTER 4

VIRTUE 2: SELFLESSNESS

Theme: How do you split the steak?

My dad and I would often split things such as dessert or a small loaf of bread. One of us would cut the food into two pieces and the other would pick which piece he wanted. This is a rather common way for families to teach fairness. As I grew older, I began to realize how selfless Dad and Mom were regarding my sisters and me. They always wanted the best for us and sacrificed for us all the time.

One day, after having spent some great time with Dad, we had a good meal of steak and a piece was left over. Dad asked me if I wanted to split it, and I said yes. He then asked me to cut it in two. For whatever reason, I understood Dad's selflessness and decided to put him to the test, because I knew how much he loved steak! I purposely cut the steak in two pieces, but instead of 50/50 I cut it 65/35. The look on Dad's face was priceless! He had to pick between what he really wanted (the big piece) and what he really wanted to teach me (selflessness)! He chose the small piece. But I stopped him as he began to move it to his plate and said, "Dad, I want you to have the big piece."

I believe that was the best tasting piece of steak either of us ever had.

Being selfless means creating the atmosphere, the processes, the training, everything about what lifts up the people you are leading. It also stems from the foundation of understanding and facilitating the dreams and goals of those you lead. Ultimately, being selfless is how those you lead learn to be selfless themselves.

Selfless: having little or no concern for oneself, especially with regard to fame, position, money, etc.; unselfish.

True selflessness means you feel joy when those you lead get the bigger piece of steak and the credit for a job well done.

For me, kindness and selflessness are similar, but there can be one significant difference. When kindness is not returned, there is seldom any physical loss on your side (you may feel emotionally hurt). Selflessness often involves physical sacrifice, but the spiritual rewards ripple through eternity.

As Les Brown suggested, "Help others achieve their dreams and you will achieve yours." As a Coach Leader, this idea is very powerful. It's simply another way of phrasing the great Zig Ziglar quote, "You can have everything in life you want if you will just help enough other people get what they want."

The key to these two powerful quotes is that your motive and your attitude toward those you lead must be selfless. These days being selfless is countercultural! It has never been more politically correct to be selfish in all the things you do. If your goal is to be an effective Coach Leader, and you approach it from a selfish mindset, the following recommendations will be of no use to you and, in fact, will make things worse for your team when you use them. Why? Because people know when they are being used or manipulated versus served and supported. Selflessness begins by serving and supporting your team, your family, and your friends.

Being selfless starts with understanding the primary needs of those you lead. A 2021 Growmotely survey of 520 remote workers revealed the top three things they look for in an employer:

1. Healthcare benefits
2. Professional development education and courses
3. Having a career/life/mindset coach

As a Coach Leader, you are perfectly positioned to provide the growth each of your team members needs. Remember, top performers can now work for anyone in the world from anywhere in the world, and they are asking, Are my leader and my organization fulfilling my needs of growing through personal and professional development education, courses, and coaching? Growth and development matter to workers.

Work-Life Balance

One of the biggest challenges over the last several decades has been the issue of work-life balance. The disruption caused by the pandemic and the future challenges that technological convergence will bring continue to highlight this issue. The way work has been done is changing. Remote and hybrid workforces continue to grow and technology is rapidly advancing. More than ever before, it is important to have a selfless mindset regarding your people. As stated earlier, it is clear that quality of life equals quality of work. A selfless mindset allows you to see the challenges facing each of your team members regarding their work-life balance.

The selfless approach means you fully understand the work-life balance needs of your team are more important than your perfect world as the leader. Ideally you might like to have your team meetings at 4:00 p.m. Pacific time because you live on the West Coast. If part of your team lives on the East Coast, this means your ideal team meeting is happening during the family dinner time for some of your people.

As you review how you lead your team, here are some fantastic ways to create this leadership virtue.

Thirteen Ways to Develop Healthy Selflessness

1. Gratitude for Your Team

Take time to create a gratitude list for each person on your team. What specific things has someone done that you are grateful for? What character qualities do they have that you appreciate? What skills and experience do they bring to the team? Take a moment to identify the overall strengths of your team and how those strengths have solved many problems. This exercise will give you a solid foundation as you realize your own success depends on your serving and supporting each person on your team and allows you to value them for who they are.

2. Knowing the Why Behind Their Why

One of the best ways to demonstrate selflessness is to really under-stand the why behind the why of the people with whom you work. The why-behind-the-why questioning process can be uncomfortable, but it is also revealing and allows you to serve and support at a deeper level. The starter question is simple: Why do you want to perform well? The answer you get will often be typical and something that anybody could say. For example, "So I can make more money." This is where the follow-up why questions dig deeper: Why do you want to make more money?

Take some time here to let them reflect on their answer. You might get a fairly short answer, but encourage them by asking, "Please tell me more." Their answer might be something like, "If I make more money, I can get out of debt." Give them an encouraging "That's great!" response and keep digging into the why. "Why do you want to get out of debt?" It's important to ask this because, after all, everybody wants to avoid debt, but what is important here is what they will do once they are out of debt. The response to this question might be, "When I get out of debt, I can really start saving." Follow that up with the next question: "Why do you want to save a lot of money?" They might answer, "So I can buy the house my wife and I have been dreaming about." The next question, "Why is buying a house so important?" They might answer, "We have always wanted to start a family, and we've been waiting until we could afford it and do it in the house that we've always wanted."

Now you have a lot of insight into the why behind the why. Can you see how this changes the nature of your relationship? After a very short conversation, your management role of maximizing a human unit of production has been transformed into a Coach Leader role of helping a person achieve their most heartfelt dream.

Now put yourself in your team member's position after you have just shared this information. How would you feel if your leader cared more about your achieving your biggest dream than they did about your hitting a certain number in production and not causing any problems? You would feel incredible! When you know the why behind the why, being selfless is far easier.

3. Understand and Foster Dream Alignment

Dream alignment begins with understanding that almost all dreams take time and money to accomplish. As a Coach Leader, when you understand their dream, their why behind the why, you can more easily connect their performance on the job to achieving their dream.

Almost every great organization recognizes that the better you perform on the job the more you are rewarded for your performance. Most of the time this recognition comes in the form of higher pay and faster promotions. One of the biggest goals for a Coach Leader is to help your people understand they are working for a dream, not a paycheck. This type of motivation is internal and enables your people to motivate themselves. When you know a team member's ultimate why is to get out of debt so they can buy a house and start a family, you can help them achieve this faster by serving and supporting them in every way possible.

Amplifying dream alignment is the next step. Most companies have a powerful mission statement and often a driving cause behind that statement. People love working for a cause and a purpose bigger than themselves. Few things are more powerful than showing someone on your team that when they perform at the highest level, the company is able to fulfill its mission statement and change lives while, at the same time, they are achieving their goals and dreams faster than they thought possible. Creating dream alignment allows you, as the Coach Leader, to demonstrate selflessness in the most powerful ways.

Many times the primary disruptions, challenges, and changes that derail dream alignment require selfless serving and support from the Coach Leader. A perfect example of this is when a team member faces a disruption that is outside the bounds of a professional working environment. It goes without saying that this disruption will impact their performance. The question is this: Are you willing to be selfless enough to serve and support your team member in a way that is outside of what is generally considered normal professional support? In my career I have witnessed selfless leaders do simple things such as go to the dry cleaners for a team member so they had an extra thirty minutes to prepare for a big presentation. This simple selfless act of service demonstrated to that team member that their leader was focused on dream alignment and not positional authority.

4. Listen

Take time to just listen. We all have things to do, deadlines to meet, and projects to complete. Being selfless is simply letting those you lead know they are more important than things or work. This doesn't mean you blow off deadlines or lower performance standards. It does mean that you are always listening for more than just the words they are saying and allowing the time to dig deeper when necessary. When you listen to understand tone, body language, and energy, this will clue you in so you can ask meaningful questions that will allow you to serve and support them even better. No one has ever complained or said, "I don't like them or respect them because they really listen to me." True listening is a selfless act, because true listening is about them and their needs and not about you.

5. Wash Their Feet

Perhaps the greatest example of selfless leadership is when Jesus washed the feet of the disciples. This was an incredible act of selflessness, as the feet of the disciples were most likely caked with the dirt, dust, and manure found on the streets two thousand years ago. Jesus said, "But whoever would be great among you must be your servant" (Matt. 20:26). Selfless Coach Leaders understand they must serve and, on occasion, "wash the feet" of their people.

To be clear, I am not suggesting you actually wash the feet of your people, but there are many daily activities you can do that fall into the highly undesirable category that demonstrates to your people your selflessness as you serve them. Perhaps a simple question such as "What are you dreading doing today?" can give you some insight into how you can better serve each team member. Of course you can't do everything for them, but what would happen if every now and then you said, "Hey, let me do that for you." Do you think by serving your people in this way they would be more likely to serve their fellow team members?

6. Give a "Nice to Have"

My oldest sister, Suzie, started a family tradition of "nice to have." Every Christmas she accompanied Dad when he would shop for a gift for Mom. Dad needed all the help he could get! On these shopping trips, Dad would tell Suzie to pick something for herself while they were shopping for Mom. Suzie suggested they also pick up some "nice to have" gifts for my sisters and me. These gifts were truly nice to have, and while they were never very expensive, they were always extremely thoughtful. After Suzie passed away in 1995, our family carried on the "nice to have" tradition. Through the years I have received many unexpected gifts from my family that were given because "I thought you would like this 'nice to have.'" What a double blessing that was! They were thinking of me and remembering Suzie at the same time.

The point of the "nice to have" is that it demonstrates thoughtfulness and action at the same time. As a Coach Leader, selflessness is thinking about your people first and often. You might already be doing this; however, your people cannot read your mind. Giving them a simple "nice to have" that is personal and to their liking is a great way to bridge the gap. Don't just get them a drink at Starbucks, get them their favorite drink. Don't just get them a thank-you card, get them a card that represents something they like. Maybe there is an inexpensive gadget you really enjoy, so pick up an extra one for someone on your team and say something as simple as, "I really enjoy this gadget and I thought you might enjoy one too." The "nice to have" is a simple demonstration of thoughtfulness that has a huge impact on your people.

7. Utilize an Open-Door Policy

Many Coach Leaders practice an open-door policy, which is simply letting your team know you always have an open door when it comes to discussing important things. This is never more critical than in times of disruption and is even more challenging with remote and hybrid workforce situations. I believe this is largely a mindset that Coach Leaders should develop within themselves. Your body language and your words should constantly communicate that you are always ready to take a needed conversation further, even if it might be uncomfortable. Far too often in the Zoom-dominated world, communication and engagement are damaged because there's not an easy way to have a hallway conversation or an end-of-the-day informal debrief.

A great approach to this challenge is to create a code word for the open-door policy that includes everyone on your team, whether they are on-site or working remotely. You can even schedule this into your calendar two or three times a week. You can call it a jam session or talk time, whatever you like. Let your people know you are available at these times to discuss whatever is on their mind or heart. When you pick up that someone on the team needs to talk or is struggling, you can simply ask, "Do you need a jam session?" The signal you are sending will come across loud and clear, and once again you are focused on their needs.

8. Activate the Disruption, Style, and Experience Mental Model

The disruption, style, and experience mental model is a powerful way to figure out how to help your people because it is focused on their needs and how you can serve and support them. Start with getting clarity on the disruption your team member is facing. Identify the facts of what's going on, and then think from their perspective how this issue is impacting their performance. Next, review in your mind their

DISC personality profile and the experiences you've had with them to understand how this specific disruption impacts their natural communication and personality style. Finally, mentally review the experiences and skills they bring to the table.

Once you have done this mental model, use this perspective to ask yourself how you can best serve and support them. This selfless response is almost the opposite of a typical response. Normally when something is disrupting a team member's performance, the leader immediately asks, how is this going to impact me and others on the team? But a Coach Leader starts from the opposite end and focuses first on the issue, the personality style, and the skills and experience of the team member. This selfless approach allows for the co-creation of a solution with the team member that has a far better chance of being implemented successfully. Remember, a primary goal of a Coach Leader is to serve, support, develop, and help grow each team member. This is best accomplished when it is clear what is currently going on and what the team member needs to improve in order to achieve the desired outcome.

9. Change Seats

When someone on your team is going through a challenge, imagine changing seats with them. Put yourself in their position. What are they thinking and feeling? What is it they're afraid of? What is it that's holding them back? Is it their mindset or skill or knowledge or the actions they are taking? Now that you're in their seat, how would you handle the challenge? Coach Leadership goes to the next level when you are truly selfless enough to view the situation from their seat.

10. Admit When You Are Wrong or Don't Know

Being selfless means you are not focused on being right but focused on discovering the truth. Because of this, there is no downside to quickly admitting when you are wrong about something or don't know the answer. Once again, your goal is to solve the problem and discover the truth, not just be right. This allows you to focus on learning and growth, which enables you to develop each team member so they can learn how to solve problems and, in the process, grow themselves. As the future brings more disruption and change, this selfless mindset will allow you to move faster and more efficiently without wasting energy. By setting an example in this area, it also allows your team members to quickly raise their hand for help and admit when they are wrong as well. This allows everyone to let go of the past and focus on the solution and to move forward without delay.

11. Give Credit and Focus on Them

A selfless Coach Leader is constantly looking for ways to identify and give credit when credit is due to each of their team members. A Coach Leader's success is completely dependent on the combined performance of each person on the team. Highlighting what team members have accomplished and how they have grown and using these examples as specific learning opportunities not only encourage team members but also equip them to do the same things when they move into leadership positions. Few things build and create the right culture and atmosphere faster than a selfless Coach Leader who is always catching the team doing something right.

12. Transform Irritation into Empathy

Have you ever thought about what irritates you and drives you nuts? Every Coach Leader is different, because you have a unique combination of personality, attitudes, and skills. Knowing your own DISC profile is a key component to understanding what drives you crazy. Now, when a team member irritates you and punches all your buttons, step back, slow down, and think about your natural personality style versus their natural personality style. Use this reflection time to transform the irritation into empathy as you understand where they're coming from. This doesn't mean you will ignore or excuse the irritation if it warrants a response. It simply means that when you address it, you will do it from a place of understanding and empathy and not from a place of condescending irritation. This is one of the most powerful and observable ways to demonstrate selflessness in your daily interactions with your team. This is truly living out patience.

13. Serve Without Personal Expectations

Serving without personal expectations might be the most difficult thing of all to do. After all, as you pour your heart into your work and into developing each person on the team, it is natural to expect reciprocation. Keep in mind there is a difference between performance expectations and personal expectations. This is not about lowering the standard of performance expectations; this is about serving your team members in a personal way as you go the extra mile without any expectation that they will return the favor. Selfless Coach Leaders never think, *If I do this for them, they will do that for me.* Instead, selfless Coach Leaders think, *If I do this for them, just imagine how much this will help them grow.* People who are growing are almost always happy and satisfied. Happy and satisfied people are far more likely to build positive and long-lasting relationships. Team members who have great relationships with their leader express gratitude toward their leader, not because they owe it, but because they are grateful. There is no better testimony for a Coach Leader than team members who are grateful for their leadership.

The following are examples of selfless acts of leadership that demonstrate many of the thirteen ways we just discussed.

Author, coach, and speaker Chris Widener shared this story:

One of the kindest things anyone ever did for me was done by an NBA star. It was 1977 and I was eleven years old. I had just gotten my dream job: towel boy for the Seattle SuperSonics (now known as the Oklahoma Thunder)! Two months after I started the job, however, I fell off a roof one afternoon while goofing around with some friends and broke both of my arms.

When I showed up for the next Sonics game, I went into the training room, where my boss, trainer Frank Furtado, was taping the ankles of Dennis Johnson, who at the time was just breaking out as a player and would win the NBA Finals MVP the next year and go on to be one of the best defensive players in league history.

Both of them looked at me and chuckled. I was funny looking with two casts up to my biceps. I asked Frank if I could keep my job. He said, "If you can do your job, you can keep it."

There wasn't much chance I was going to be able to do my job, because the first thing I had to do every game when I got there was to make two five-gallon jugs of Gatorade and haul them two hundred yards to courtside.

I went into the room to make the Gatorade and barely got it done. While I was making it, DJ came in and told me to drag the jugs outside the locker room (so Frank could see me doing my job) and wait for him to do his shootaround and warm-ups. So I did. It was all I could do to drag those jugs twenty feet outside the doors of the locker room, let alone two hundred yards to the court.

After a few minutes, out walked DJ. He handed me a basketball and said, "Carry this." Then he picked up both jugs and carried them to the court for me . . . for the next six weeks while my arms healed. His selfless act of kindness enabled me to keep that job, a job I would have for seven years and was one of the highlights of my life.

Looking back, what made this even more amazing is that the first hundred yards was through underground tunnels, but then the doors opened to a concourse where the players had to walk through all the fans to get to the court. Every game for six weeks, DJ humbled himself and let the fans see him carrying the jugs of Gatorade so a little kid could keep his dream job.

This to me shows the spirit of Martin Luther King's message: Kindness among the races. Love. Service. Humility.

DJ passed away a few years ago from a heart attack while he was coaching, but he left a profound impact on my life and how we should treat one another, regardless of the color of our skin.

My longtime friend Brian Miller shared this story with me:

I have seen a lot of selflessness over the years as an owner of a company and as a veteran, but one story comes to mind, and it was actually me that did the act. It was around 1997. I was going to school, working full time, and serving in the National Guard. My wife was pregnant, and we already had two little ones, ages four and two. I was a supervisor at a telemarketing company in charge of several hundred employees.

About a month before Christmas, a young lady came to me. (I'm sorry, I can't remember her name, but I will never forget what happened.) She said she needed to work overtime the next month and would like a raise. I could see she was upset, and I asked her what was wrong. She broke down in tears. She said she was going to jail in a month, right after Christmas. She said she helped raise her brother because her dad was not around, and her mother was working two jobs and was also on drugs. She said he was always getting into trouble, and this time he had killed a person. She tried to get him to leave, but he was sobbing and hiding from the police. She couldn't turn him away. So she hid him. The police found him, and he went to jail, and she was convicted for aiding and abetting a criminal and received an eighteen-month sentence. She cried, "I have a fifteen-month-old. I just want to give my baby a good Christmas before I go! My baby will go to foster care, because none of my family will step up, and I will have to fight to get her back when I get out."

I was deeply saddened by this and went to the boss, and, of course, he said no. Later that night I went home and told my wife the situation. We were broke, I mean living-on-mac-and-cheese-and-ramen-noodles broke, but I felt as if I needed to do something. I asked MaryLee, my wife, if I could give this girl a hundred dollars. She said okay. Now, a hundred dollars doesn't sound like much, but back then, it was a ton of money to us.

The next morning I called the employee into my office. I explained the company did not want to give out overtime or a raise. I then said, "I still want to help you. I know it isn't much, but here is a hundred dollars." You would have thought I gave her a winning lottery ticket.

She burst into tears and hugged me for a very long time. I received something hard to explain from that moment. It was like God smiling. It truly felt like I was the one receiving a gift. I don't know if she thinks about this anymore, but all I know is how I felt after that moment. It was one of the best feelings I have ever felt, and I still think about it once in a while, especially around the holidays. You truly can have everything in life you want, if you will just help enough other people get what they want.

Jim Gardner is a coach, speaker, consultant, and a longtime friend. He told me the following story:

Last year I was competing on a team in a Tough Mudder in Colorado. One of our teammates, an army veteran, has one leg, the other was amputated at the hip. This teammate was determined to participate in and complete the three-and-a-half-mile, fifteen-obstacle race on crutches.

About a half mile into the race and after the third obstacle, our army veteran teammate had rubbed blisters on his underarms and the palms of his hands. But he wasn't about to quit.

One of my teammates is a fitness trainer. He said, "We started as a team, we will finish as a team, leaving no one behind."

The fitness trainer then carried, over his shoulders, the army veteran between each of the remaining obstacles, approximately three miles, at altitude in Colorado. This was something no one else on our team would have been physically capable of doing.

There were over twelve thousand competitors in this Tough Mudder race. Shortly after the trainer began carrying the army vet, the other competitors began to notice this selfless act. A roar of clapping and cheering began to build.

By the time our team crossed the finish line, there were thousands of competitors from other teams cheering and crying with joy as they witnessed real leadership and self-sacrifice in real time.

Our team could have finished this race faster had we left our army vet after the third obstacle. But no one could have finished better that day after having experienced what is most important in life: carrying your brother when he is not able to carry himself.

Steve Collins, a Ziglar Legacy certified speaker and coach, told me this story:

Craig Owen, my longtime friend and owner of our San Antonio office, brought me on as a coach five years ago. He knew that my goal was to pass on the Ziglar legacy and ultimately leave the company to serve a larger number of people around the world. He has done everything in his power to support my departure to the next phase of life, even though, by God's grace, I have been able to make a significant impact on the productivity and culture of our office over the last five years. He knew from the beginning I would be leaving, and he has been supportive and helpful throughout the process.

As you reflect on these stories of selflessness, take some time to review the thirteen specific ways you can demonstrate selflessness to those you serve and lead. As you think about the following questions, write down your three choices from the list of thirteen that you will grow in yourself to help demonstrate the answer to each question.

- What specific things can you intentionally focus on each day to build selflessness in yourself?
- What specific things can you do for those you serve and lead that will demonstrate selflessness to them?
- How can you encourage other leaders in your organization to become more selfless in their approach?

Chapter 5

VIRTUE 3: RESPECT

Theme: Give it to get it.

By wise guidance you can wage your war,
and in abundance of counselors there is victory.

—Proverbs 24:6

When I was growing up, it was made clear to me that one of the best ways to respect other people was through our language. Common courtesy and respect were taught to me through the words my parents used. I was never allowed to speak negatively of myself or anyone else. Profanity of any kind was not tolerated, and neither were words spoken out of anger. The power of the tongue was well known and deeply respected in our home for its ability to heal and to harm.

When I started working for our company, I had the opportunity to travel with Dad when he spoke for corporate clients. My job was to carry the bags and sell the books and audio programs at the back of the room when Dad was finished speaking. I also attended some fancy dinners and was invited into the greenroom before Dad would speak. This allowed me to meet some successful and influential people from all walks of life. In almost every case, the leadership of these large companies demonstrated courtesy, hospitality, and respect to everyone I saw them communicate with. Dad and I had many conversations about how these leaders treated other people. I learned quickly from Dad that he respected people who respected people.

On one trip with Dad, we were invited to a small gathering of the top company leadership of a very successful oil and gas company. I could tell that many of the executives had worked their way up through the organization over many years. These were loyal, long-term team players who had invested the majority of their lives in this company. I could also tell they knew each other well. But something else stood out to me as well: they took cussing to a whole new level! Growing up in a home and working in a business where profanity didn't exist, well, this was a shock to me.

After we had been there a while, I had a private moment with Dad and mentioned all the cussing. I will never forget what he told me. "Son, never mistake the words that someone uses as a sign of lack of intelligence or education. This room is filled with smart people who we can learn a lot from, and based on the track records they have, it's obvious they have done well in life. However, isn't it a shame that without even knowing it, they are alienating some people by the words they choose to use?"

This was the first time in a business environment I realized firsthand how essential it is to respect other people, even if their language, education, or culture was different from mine. One of the things a Coach Leader can do is look for things in each team member that are worthy of respect.

Somebody Is Always Watching

Showing respect to others is always a good practice. How you treat other people, especially those who are there to serve, says everything about you and sets a powerful example. Mom and Dad would often go to Luby's Cafeteria. (I jokingly tell people I was weaned at Luby's!) In fact, going to Luby's was like eating at home. When we walked in, Mom would hug the cashier, who she knew by name, and ask about her family. As we went down the cafeteria line, Dad would give each server a brief word of encouragement and ask them how they were doing and about their families. When I was a teenager, I would roll my eyes as this happened, but as an adult, I realized that Dad's plate had extraordinarily large servings of whatever he had ordered. This became an issue and Dad had to ask them to stop scooping so much food onto his plate! Years later, I still encounter people who watched Dad and Mom as they treated every server and employee in the cafeteria with such respect and as if they were family. As a Coach Leader, if you want your team members to treat each other with respect, it starts with how you treat everyone you encounter.

Respect Doesn't Always Mean Agreement

One of the disruptions and challenges we face in today's business climate is the rise of the cancel culture. Far too often, people are automatically demeaned because of a difference of opinion. This is the ultimate disrespect. Respect is acknowledging the basic right for someone else to have an opinion and beliefs that are different from yours. The Coach Leader understands that you cannot gain respect by disrespecting others. Respecting someone does not automatically mean that you agree with their beliefs and opinions, but it simply means you acknowledge that they have them.

Many years ago our company had a training contract with a very large government organization. We were called in to work on team building and customer service for the employees who worked in the dozens of toll booths that managed the parking facilities at that location. Customers would pay for parking on a time-used basis, receiving a time-stamped receipt on the way in and then paying a fee on the way out, based on how much time they had been parked at the site.

Krish Dhanam on our team was head of this training project. As he did his due diligence and created a customized training program, he discovered there was a rift between many of the toll-booth employees. The fundamental rift involved the employees' perspective on their jobs. The toll booth operators had to talk to the people, take their tolls, and often sort through the issue of a lost toll receipt, which regularly led to heated interactions with the customers. The working conditions were subject to the weather, meaning the operators were exposed to extreme heat, rain, and extreme cold because it was necessary to keep the window and the door open in order to serve the customers.

The rift between the employees involved how difficult the job was and was divided along culture lines. About half of the employees were immigrants from all over the world. This job was often their first step to living out the American dream. Many of them couldn't believe they actually had a private office. They were amazed that their private office had a fan and heater as well as a covering to mitigate the challenges with the weather. As a group they were grateful that they had the opportunity for this job.

The other half were regular citizens. They wanted to see an improvement in workplace conditions, and they didn't like the fact that others in the organization were making the same amount of money but weren't exposed to the harsh elements of the weather as they were. When these issues were brought up in team meetings, neither side could understand the perspective of the other, because all they were focused on was their own perspective.

When Krish created the training program around team building, he decided to ignore the buzzword of the time, which was cultural diversity, and he instead focused on a term he created, "cultural similarity." When Krish explained the program to me, it was partially based on his own experience as an immigrant from India.

Krish arrived in the United States with nine dollars in his pocket and immediately found work in the pursuit of his American dream. Krish was 100 percent awestruck by the opportunity he saw in front of him compared to what he had left behind, just as many of the immigrants working in the toll booths were.

Krish let me know he was going to focus on the cultural similarities and values that both groups shared in order to build a bridge to unite the team. Respect was the core similarity that laid the foundation for this training. Krish knew that wanting to be respected is a universal trait. By asking everyone in the training class what they valued and how they wanted to be treated, it became clear they all wanted the same thing. The rift occurred because they had not taken the time to understand the others' perspective, experience, and upbringing.

Just like Krish, as a Coach Leader you have to be ready for how the people you lead will respond to disruption, challenge, and change. Many times the disconnect you feel in your team stems from team members' lack of understanding and respect for each other. As the leader you have a responsibility to demonstrate and create respect throughout your team and your business. The following are ten ways to create, show, and grow respect in your organization.

Ten Ways to Create, Show, and Grow Respect

1. Respect yourself. Respect starts with respecting yourself. Do you respect yourself enough to intentionally grow and develop every area of your life? Are you daily working on your mindset and your spiritual and physical health? Are you actively moving toward your purpose and building relationships with other people who value and respect you and want the best for you? Is your self-talk positive and uplifting? Are you your biggest supporter? Do you expect more, less, or the same from yourself as you do from others? Have you defined healthy boundaries for your own life? Do you advocate for yourself just as you do for others? Coach Leaders understand that respect from others is often a response to how others see them respecting themselves.

2. Define what respect means to you. What does respect mean to you? Take time to create a list of how you know you are being respected. Does respect to you mean that people listen intently, show up on time, give you credit when credit is due, acknowledge you even when they don't really know you? Write this list down and focus on the feelings you have when people show respect to you. Now compare this list to the ways listed here and ask yourself, If I treat others the way I want to be treated, with respect, will they feel respected? As you study this question you will learn that, as a Coach Leader, there may be some ways you need to treat others that are beyond the way you want to be treated.

3. Communicate and listen. Do you communicate and listen to others in the way they want to be communicated to and listened to? As we covered earlier, everyone has a particular personality style and a specific way they like to be communicated to. One of the best ways to show respect is through active listening and intentional questions. Being 100 percent present with engaged body language and curious questions shows the other person they have your attention. There are few things that show more respect than this. As you listen, keep in mind that you are listening to understand more than you are listening to share your own knowledge. This active listening, with intentional questions, will give you great insight into what the other person is thinking and feeling. When you combine this with an understanding of communication styles, such as the DISC personality profile, you can tailor your conversation to a person's most attentive ear. This approach shows respect because it acknowledges that you are communicating in the way they like to be communicated to rather than the way you like to communicate. This shows respect by letting them know they are important.

4. See their perspective. One of the best ways to show respect is to look at a situation from the other person's perspective. Before an important coaching conversation, it is a great preparation strategy to do a mental model of how you want the conversation to go. A mental model is simply a series of questions you ask yourself regarding the conversation you are about to have. What outcome do you want? What is the other person thinking and feeling? What unique ideas and perspectives does the other person have regarding the situation? What are the strengths and weaknesses of the other person? What barriers and what types of resources does the other person have or need to be successful? What questions can I ask the other person to better understand their perspective? All these questions allow you to better see the perspective the other person brings to the table. One of the benefits of understanding a team member's perspective is that you can support them as they set goals for their own growth. Understanding where someone is coming from allows you to better guide them toward where they want to go. In fact, people are often hesitant to take your direction until they know you care about where they are coming from.

5. Ask questions (go first). Showing respect means that you go first. This starts with a greeting, a welcome, a handshake, and all the social outreach that makes someone feel welcome. Going first is about asking the questions that make someone feel appreciated. The best way to do this is by asking open-ended questions that you follow up with more open-ended questions.

Bob Tiede, my friend and mentor, observed, "Leadership is not as much about knowing the right answers as it is about asking the right questions!" And he wrote an excellent book titled *Now That's a Great Question*, which has dozens of example questions you can ask. When asking questions, always remember the purpose behind each question is to better understand the person and the situation so you can more effectively serve them and discover the best way to solve problems and uncover the truth.

6. Celebrate. Gratitude is one of the healthiest of all human emotions, and one of the best ways to show gratitude to your team is to celebrate their successes. The celebration does not need to be huge and elaborate, but it does need to be meaningful and specific. When you take a few moments to specifically acknowledge a job well done, either by an individual or the team, you let them know they are valued and respected. In the celebration you need to be specific about what was accomplished and, if possible, how and why it was accomplished.

Everyone loves recognition, especially when it is specific to what they did. You can take the celebration and the respect to the next level by also making it meaningful. This can be done in two ways. First, the recognition should reflect the way the individual likes to be recognized, meaning you need to consider their personality type. An extrovert might love a team meeting, a chance to talk, and some food to celebrate with. An introvert might prefer an email copied to the team and to company leadership. Second, the recognition should connect what was accomplished directly to the character qualities the person displayed in achieving the accomplishment. It is good to celebrate the results. It is more than good to celebrate how the results were achieved. Never forget that recognizing someone incorrectly can be as bad as not recognizing them at all.

7. Keep your word. The number-one key to a Coach Leader's long-term success is integrity. The way your team and your business will ultimately judge your integrity is by how well you keep your word. Respect is gained and lost not only by what you say but also by what you don't say. Keeping your word starts with how you define integrity and your commitment in every communication and relationship.

What is your word? It is not only what you say and the promises you make but also the standards you set. If you choose to adopt the ten virtues described in this book as the foundation on which to build your career as a Coach Leader, then you will need to live by them as well as call out those on your team and in your business who violate these ten virtues. Far too many times, respect is lost because leaders do not hold others to the same standard they hold themselves. This is especially true in a business environment, when leaders publicly express what they believe but let others on their team violate these beliefs without any consequences. Your word and the standard you set must be honored by you at all times or it will have no real respect.

> "When your word is no good, you are no good."
>
> *—Zig Ziglar*

8. Scale trust. Several years ago I had the opportunity to meet with Seth Godin. Prior to our meeting, I did some research on what he was focused on, and I discovered his concept of the "scalability of trust." When I asked him what the scalability of trust meant, he said, "In every interaction, trust is either growing or diminishing."

When we have a conversation with a team member, send an email, post on social media, turn in a project, deliver a product or service, the receiver of that information either has an increased or a decreased level of trust in us. Because of this, Seth told me that our goal should be to increase trust in every interaction. More trust means better relationships and opens doors for all types of business to occur. Whenever we take a shortcut and undermine our word or fail in a commitment, we are eroding trust. The more trust erodes, the more the relationship erodes—and the less likely business will be done.

In the book *Secrets of Closing the Sale*, Zig Ziglar wrote there are five reasons people do not buy: no need, no money, no hurry, no want, and no trust. The biggest reason they don't buy, though, is no trust. Seth explained in our conversation that, by establishing trust, we have overcome their biggest objection to doing business, and all that's left is to find a solution that fits their needs. Take a moment to examine this concept as a Coach Leader. You may not be selling a product or a service to your team, but you are constantly selling ideas, common goals, and a vision. Are you scaling trust with every conversation you have with your team and in your business? Can you have a meaningful relationship without trust? Can you have trust without integrity?

9. No gossip—ever! Gossip is the little thing that can, over time, destroy respect on a team and for a leader. Gossip is simply talking negatively about someone or something to someone who has no power or ability to fix the situation. Because gossip is used by people to build themselves up at the expense of someone else, it is a sure way to lose respect. When you are known as someone who will gossip, the others on your team will no longer trust you with information that is essential during times of disruption. A Coach Leader understands from the beginning that if what is being said doesn't benefit the people involved and solve the problem, then it shouldn't be said at all. Living by and making your team a no-gossip zone creates an atmosphere of trust and respect. No one likes to worry about what is being said behind their back.

One more thing about gossip. When gossip is done on social media, it goes nuclear, and the fallout can ruin a career. Don't do it.

As a Coach Leader, set the example in your own social media and be ready to cover your views on it with the team.

10. Let your virtues lead your actions. Being kind and looking for the best in a selfless way creates deep and long-lasting respect. As a Coach Leader, if you only remember one thing about showing, creating, and gaining respect, it would be this: be kind. Kindness has an incredible ability to bring out the best in people. Sometimes, as a Coach Leader, respect has to be reestablished because someone on the team has either purposely or unintentionally been disrespectful. Being kind is a powerful way to defuse the situation and can also be the standard you establish that helps people repair rocky relationships. Disrespect is often shown in body language and tone more than in confrontation. This subtle disrespect is often overlooked, and this usually leads to a major disruption. One way to avoid this is to set the kindness standard early and high with your team.

Let your team know you will act and communicate with them in kindness in every situation, regardless of the emotions involved, and that you expect the same. This way, when someone on the team shows disrespect by eye-rolling or overtalking, you can have a private coaching conversation with them. A simple way to approach this conversation is to ask them what's going on as soon as you notice this behavior. Let them explain and then let them know the reason you are bringing it up is because it is a sign of disrespect, and you want to make sure that wasn't the case. After their response, drive the point home by saying, "One of our team values is kindness," and then ask them how that behavior reflects kindness. Shaunti Feldhahn observed, "Kindness is more than just being kind; it is stopping behaviors that are unkind." Respect and kindness go hand-in-hand. It is impossible to be kind and disrespectful at the same time.

Looking for the best is lived out by giving credit and making it personal. One way to build respect is to let people know you respect them for their character, integrity, principles, and values. Many people give lip service to this idea, but it takes on a much deeper meaning when it is tied to specific, observable behavior.

Suppose a team member is working on a project with an account. Just before the deadline, the team member comes to you and says they have discovered a problem and it could delay the delivery of the project and they want to make you aware of it. The team member then calls in the others who are working on the project to explain the issue, and the team goes about solving it. This team member, without anyone's knowledge, spends all night fixing all the issues with the problem. The next day you have a recap meeting with the team member and start to dig into what the team member has done and you are very impressed.

The typical way credit would be given in this example would be to say, "Great job," and then acknowledge them in front of their peers for going above and beyond what was expected. But as a Coach Leader you know you can affirm, acknowledge, and celebrate the results in a much more powerful way. You do this by specifically identifying the character qualities the team member exhibited in solving the problem. This can be done verbally one-on-one, in a team meeting, or even in an email. Regardless of the means, the key is to thank the top performer for setting a high standard and working with the others in a difficult situation with kindness and respect.

A Coach Leader never passes up an opportunity to give credit, especially when the core values of the person align with the company's values, and this is the reason for the success of the project.

Engagement, Collaboration, and Creativity

One of the most significant challenges facing today's Coach Leader is creating an atmosphere where engagement, collaboration, and creativity abound. The accelerated pace of change, combined with the hybrid workforce, has made it extremely difficult to create an environment that allows for teams to do their best work. Without mutual respect from all the members of the team, it is impossible over a long period of time to keep the team engaged, collaborating, and innovating.

Below are two practical ways to show, grow, and create respect with your team and increase engagement, collaboration, and creativity.

1. Appreciation, Inspiration, Recognition (AIR)

Everyone, and especially a high-performing team, needs AIR (appreciation, inspiration, and recognition). When you provide your team with pure AIR, respect grows exponentially. A best practice for your team meetings could be to start the agenda with AIR. Set aside the first five to ten minutes of your team meeting to follow this simple procedure. As the Coach Leader you will need to go first, and then as the team grows comfortable with the exercise, you can ask others to contribute as well. Here is the four-step agenda item written as if *you* are leading the AIR exercise.

Step 1: Introduction. Welcome to our meeting today. Let's get started. I want to begin this team meeting with AIR, and of course everyone knows that AIR stands for appreciation, inspiration, and recognition.

Step 2: Appreciation. I want to start by appreciating John for coming in early today and getting everything set up. That makes my life easier and makes the day go better for everyone on the team. Thanks, John, for what you do. Who else would like to show some appreciation for someone on the team?

Give one or two others a chance to talk and appreciate someone else and more if it's going well. (Total time: two to three minutes.)

Step 3: Inspiration. I found a quote I want to share with you that I try to live by: "You can have everything in life you want if you will just help enough other people get what they want." Zig Ziglar said this, and I really believe it. In my own life I have discovered that when I am focused on solving the problems of other people, rather than focusing on my own needs, I am much more successful and happier. I am grateful for each of you and how you also live out this quote and how we work together as a team.

You can tell a story, read part of a book, use a quote, play a song, anything that inspires the group to a higher standard. You can also ask team members in advance to provide the inspiration, as everyone understands this part of the agenda better. (Total time: two to four minutes.)

Step 4: Recognition. I want to take a moment to recognize Becky for a job well done. Yesterday you landed the Baker account, and I know you have been working on that for several months. You did a beautiful job on the proposal and were very creative with the solutions that were offered. I am especially pleased with how you presented our values and sold the benefits of working with us. This took a lot of conviction and courage on your part, because by not lowering the price, there was a risk of the client saying no to the proposal. Your belief in our products and services allows us to deliver a world-class solution with integrity, because we have the margin to give the account 100 percent support.

You can also ask others on the team if they want to recognize someone else on the team who has done a great job or helped them specifically with a project or problem.

2. Team Meetings Are Inclusive, Respectful, and Everyone Is Allowed to Be Heard

The second practical way of creating respect on your team has to do with how you run your meetings. The landmark Google Aristotle project on building effective teams discovered the three key components of great teams.[5] The *how* is essential in every meeting and even more important when people are not in the same room together. As a Coach Leader, here are the three keys to making sure that respect is created and you are getting the greatest benefit out of your team meetings.

Key 1: Everyone on your team must feel included in the team meeting. If you are physically together in the same room, this means that everyone is sitting at the table. In a blended or remote team environment, it's critical that everyone is invited who needs to be in the meeting, and it is worth considering inviting those who may not have an active role to play in the meeting but still need to know what's going on. Leaving people out of the meeting for practical reasons may be logical, but in a blended workforce it can lead to feelings of isolation.

Additional things to consider include setting the standard for participation and engagement. I highly recommend that all cameras are on and everyone is able to see an active engagement, even when they are participating from off-site. Chatting and sharing documents, with team members contributing during the meeting, are other ways to create inclusion and engagement. The benefit of video, audio, and the written word is that this allows individual preferences for communication to shine. A great way to make introverts feel included is to allow them to contribute via chat or shared document, and then ask them to explain what they've written. As a Coach Leader, you will have to determine the right balance and frequency for your meetings. Not including people and having too few meetings leads to disengagement and isolation. Having too many meetings that take more time than they should leads to exhaustion and loss of productivity. Because of this, it is essential that every meeting has an agenda and each person knows their role and what's expected of them in the meeting before they attend. The key thing to remember is that agenda-driven meetings are far more effective if everyone on the team is included.

Key 2: Everyone feels welcome and safe. Respect is built in team interactions when everyone feels safe about contributing and sharing ideas and information with their team. Many times this requires courage and vulnerability from team members, especially when they are admitting they need help in finding a solution. If team members feel attacked or spoken down to by others on the team, they will not share their need for help or their ideas for possible solutions. As a Coach Leader, you need to establish from the beginning what respect looks like in a team meeting, and this includes verbal tone and physical gestures. Nothing will shut down a team member faster than a harsh or condescending tone, combined with eye-rolling and gestures of disrespect. A Coach Leader must lead by example, sharing appropriate vulnerabilities, and recognizing that they don't have all the answers to every problem. If necessary, the Coach Leader will take control of the meeting if discussion becomes too intense and will follow up with private coaching conversations with the concerned team members.

Key 3: Everyone is heard. This concept is critically important, especially in smaller teams, where it would be normal for everyone to speak at some point during the meeting. Successful teams rely on every member of the team to contribute; however, not everyone's personality or style makes it easy for them to contribute. As the Coach Leader your goal is to have each team member speak up and contribute to each meeting.

A great way to manage this expectation is to have in front of you the name of each person in the meeting. As you progress through the meeting agenda, put a checkmark by a person's name each time they speak. Halfway through the meeting look to see who has not yet spoken. As you move forward in the meeting, ask engaging questions to those who have not spoken so you can get their input as well. For example, "Lisa, I can tell you're thinking about this situation. What do you think we should do or what would you like to add or how do you see this working in your area?" This type of engagement question shows respect to everyone in the meeting.

Someone who is new or doesn't work directly on a project might not have much to add, but often their perspective is what turns a good idea into a great idea. By respecting everyone in the meeting and getting their engagement, you create buy-in to whatever decisions are made. Everyone appreciates being heard and people also understand that not every recommendation will be put into action. Remember, when people are shown the respect of being asked and heard, they are far more likely to support the course of action determined by the leader.

As a Coach Leader, you understand and believe you have to give respect in order to get it. Respect is about acknowledging the value of each person. Everyone has their own perspective and experiences, and while our opinions and beliefs may differ, we respect each person's right to have them. Coach Leaders know that breakthroughs and innovations are usually born out of fresh and different perspectives, and respect allows these perspectives to be shared rather than hidden.

Here are three questions to consider regarding respect:

- What can I do today that will allow me to respect myself more?
- How can I show, create, and build respect with and between my team members?
- How can I more visibly respect my leaders?

CHAPTER 6

VIRTUE 4: HUMILITY

Theme: Do not be proud or arrogant.

Being humble, combined with curiosity, builds bridges and solves problems. Questions are the answers, and the power of the question depends on the humility of the leader. C. S. Lewis observed, "Humility is not thinking less of yourself; it is thinking of yourself less."

In 2019, I was invited to speak at Youngstown State University in Ohio. This event was made possible by Greg Smith and was hosted by Adam Earnheardt. In one of the sessions, I asked the group what the opposite of gratitude was. I have asked many groups this question, and this was the first time someone answered it correctly *and* on the first try.

A young lady said, "Entitlement."

Humility allows you to be grateful for what you have.

Arrogance creates entitlement and makes you resent what you don't have.

Humility and gratitude are inextricably entwined.

Zig Ziglar said, "The more you are grateful for what you have, the more you will have to be grateful for."

Gratitude allows you to focus on what you have in times of disruption.

Entitlement makes you fixate on how unfair things are because of what you don't have in times of disruption.

I am starting this chapter by juxtaposing *gratitude* with *entitlement* because, in the business world, far too often, immature leaders do not see the return on investment in humility. Mature Coach Leaders, however, understand that humility and gratitude are key foundation stones when disruption comes. Our culture is based on performance, which typically means our value (and unfortunately our self-worth) usually goes hand-in-hand with our results. This drives competitiveness and an unhealthy projection of pride and arrogance. The "fake it till you make it" swagger turns into a judgmental disposition toward anyone who has not "earned" respect. When you bluff your way through your insecurities and lack of experience and knowledge, you begin to assume everyone else is doing the same. Arrogance manifests itself in masking what you don't know and then focuses on exposing what others don't know. Arrogance means you argue to win rather than question to discover the truth. If you are highly talented and experienced, this approach often gets great results—until everything changes. Arrogant leaders are fine with climbing the ladder by stepping on others.

Humility is a completely different approach to leadership. Humble leaders relish the fact that they don't know everything. Why? Because if they knew everything, they would be done growing. The change and disruption that is coming will only be embraced and solved proportionate to your ability to learn and grow. Humility allows you to recognize quickly that you don't have the answer, but you likely know the people who do.

As a Coach Leader, ask yourself the following questions from a position of humility:

- How do you view your peers and those you lead?
- Are you grateful for their skills and experiences?
- Do you focus on their strengths or on their weaknesses?
- Are you convinced your job is to persuade them of your point of view?
- Are you curious about their perspectives, beliefs, and recommendations?

How you answer these questions tells you a lot about your mindset toward those around you, regarding your own humility and arrogance.

Can you be humble and confident at the same time? Yes!

Being humble doesn't mean weakness or lacking confidence. In fact, a synonym for *humility* is *meekness*, which means power with restraint. If a three-year-old threatens to beat you up, do you get fearful and defend yourself or do you smile, laugh, and pick them up and hug them? Being humble flows from knowing who you are, understanding your strengths and shortcomings, and owning the responsibility to learn and grow in the areas that are holding you down. Getting ahead is not about pushing others back but about growing yourself.

Short-term confidence (arrogance) is built on what you have accomplished and requires you to constantly get wins.

Long-term confidence (humility) is built on knowing that you know the process of learning and solving problems and that you don't need to know everything; you just need to know what questions to ask and who to ask.

The difference between short- and long-term confidence is one of the biggest lessons the COVID-19 pandemic has taught us. Many seemingly strong leaders lost their ability to lead because the disruption was so great that the short-term wins necessary to keep their self-confidence up stopped happening. These leaders, out of arrogance, felt as if it were their lone responsibility to come up with the answers to problems they couldn't solve. When a leader's self-confidence is the primary way they inspire confidence within the team, it only takes a moment for the team to lose confidence when the leader loses confidence.

Humility understands that long-term confidence is built by doing the right things in the right way. Coach Leaders know long-term confidence is created through relationships built on character and integrity and on the belief that powerful, curious questions fuel collaboration, creativity, and the co-creation of innovative solutions to the most difficult challenges. Humility is eager to give credit where credit is due and celebrates everyone's contribution.

Technology's Impact

Humility will play an essential role in your ability to embrace the massive changes that are coming because of the advances in technology. In *The Future Is Faster Than You Think*,[6] Peter H. Diamandis and Steven Kotler discuss the concept of technological convergence. Massive technological advances are rolling out even as you're reading this book:

- Blockchain will change the way business is done.
- 5G is up to a hundred times faster than 4G.
- Quantum computing is 100 trillion times faster than classical computing.

- AI is advancing rapidly and changing the face of business.
- Battery storage technology is making *The Jetsons* a reality.

Each of these technologies will radically change the way we work and live. Convergence is when these technologies come together and have an exponential impact. In November 2020, I started the refinance process on our home to take advantage of historically low interest rates. I had to provide more than fifty documents to get approval and it took almost ninety days. To make it even more frustrating, my loan was for only 40 percent of the value of the home, with no cash out. Government regulations designed to protect me instead cost me money and lots of hair! Technologists believe in the near future this type of financial transaction will be done through blockchain technology. Simply put, each person will have their own secure blockchain wallet, where all your confidential information can be safely stored. It is believed that a record of every financial transaction you have ever made will be stored in this location. Every purchase, paycheck, tax bill, withdrawal, and payment to or from you will be recorded and saved.

As a result, getting a home loan will go forward in the following manner:

- You apply for a loan.
- The lender requests access to your blockchain financial records.
- Ten minutes later you will receive an email with the news your old loan has been paid off and your new loan has the following included payment details.

The convergence of AI, blockchain, 5G, and supercomputing without human interaction will do in less than ten minutes what now takes a team of people ninety days to do.

Humalogy

The word *humalogy* was coined by Scott Klososky, the founder of Future Point of View (FPOV). Humalogy is a framework for describing the blending of humans and technology. During the writing of this book, I had several discussions with Scott regarding the changes technology is bringing to leaders. He described the concept of humalogy and an easy-to-understand scale to see where the future is heading. The scale has 10 points. The first point on the left end of the scale is labeled H5 and the point on the far right is labeled T5. H5 signifies a completely human function, and as you move from left to right, the function shifts from human to technology, with T5 being a completely technological function. The middle of the scale is represented as a zero (0) and signifies a 50/50 relationship between human and technology.

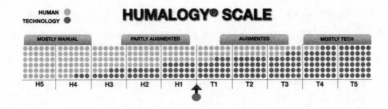

Reflect on your own work experience and where you see humalogy going in your business. Not long ago we would make a phone call and talk to a receptionist, who would transfer the call to the person we wanted to talk to. Now we make a call and have to respond to a robotic menu with little chance of actually talking to a human. In the near future an AI-driven voice will answer our questions, and we will never talk to a human being, but we will think we are. This is an example of the humalogy scale at work.

Humility, Humalogy, and Coach Leaders

I asked Scott what leaders should be preparing for regarding the changes coming with technology. He said leaders should understand the need to embrace technology in order to effectively lead in the new world. Older and more experienced leaders are often reluctant to embrace new technology to help them lead more effectively. Now, with more and more people working from home or in a hybrid work environment, opportunities for face-to-face brainstorming meetings focused on creativity and innovation are less frequent. However, new collaboration technologies are being created that can make innovation far more likely in a remote setting. Leaders who understand this and have the humility to let go of their old ways and learn something new will have a huge advantage. It takes courage and humility to try something new and potentially look like a novice in front of the younger people you lead, who adapt so readily to new technology.

Humility encourages and enables you to ask life-changing questions about yourself and about others, such as, What is keeping me from having maximum impact?

Just like the collaboration technology example above, it is a great practice to identify the problems holding you and your team back and then embrace learning the solution, even though it will be uncomfortable. There have been numerous times in my speaking career when I have been asked to present to an audience that wasn't my ideal fit. Arrogance would have said, "Most people like your talk just the way it is, so it's up to them to embrace it the way you like to do it." Instead, I became intentional about why I was there in the first place: it's not about me, it's about them!

My goal is to have the greatest impact possible, and I do this by accepting the facts around an event (such as the audience is made up of young people, senior citizens, PhDs) and peculiar limitations (such as having only fifteen minutes for the presentation or being the last speaker at the end of a grueling four-day event). Once I ask the questions and understand the facts, I can focus on some solutions that will allow for the greatest impact. I don't like being the last speaker at the end of a long day, but that may be the situation. Given this, how can I energize the crowd and change my presentation for maximum impact? It's a given I don't know everything and the circumstances aren't ideal, but my choice was how I approached the solution. When I started with humility (this is about them, not me), I could ask the right questions and come up with the best solutions. This is the approach every Coach Leader should take.

Who Do I Know Who Can Do This Better than I Can?

Several years ago I was having breakfast with my friend and mentor Bob Tiede. He is an expert on questions, so any time we get together, I know he is going to help me to discover something new through his questions.

His opening question that morning was, "How are you doing?"

I told him I was doing well overall and the company was doing well, but I was feeling overwhelmed.

He then asked the usual follow-up question, "Can you tell me more?"

I said that the days were packed with so much to do and that we were going through a lot of changes, and this just left me overwhelmed.

And then he repeated the question, "Can you tell me a little bit more?"

I said that my frustration with being overwhelmed was that people would bring me great ideas that I knew we should do, but I just didn't have the bandwidth to do them, and this really frustrated me.

Bob said, "You're asking yourself the wrong question. The question shouldn't be 'How do I do this?' The question should be 'Who should do this?' You see, most of the time, there is someone better than you to solve the problem or implement the good idea, and it's your job to pass it to them."

Understanding this concept is a game changer. Humility allows you to take responsibility, not for doing the task and assuming you are the only one with the answer, but for finding the best person to do it.

What Do They Know That I Can Learn from Them?

Imagine you've been assigned a project with huge implications and a short timeline in an area about which you only have a general understanding. But on your team is a new person who you know has a great deal of information in this area from a previous job. What do you do?

Do you hand them the project and say, "Get 'er done!"?

Do you tell them exactly how you want them to do it and then micromanage them?

Do you come up with a series of questions such as

- Have you done a project like this before?
- How did it turn out?
- What challenges did you face?
- Knowing what you know, can you put a plan together for this project?
- How can I help you?

Of course, the series of questions is the way to go. And yet we pass up this opportunity every day with the people we've been successfully working with for months or even years. What if you asked them questions such as:

- I'm curious. How or where did you learn to do it that way?
- What other ways of doing it did you consider but reject? Why?
- I know we had limited time or limited money on this project. If we didn't, what would you have done differently?
- What are you most proud of regarding this project?
- What frustrated you about this project?

These questions work best when they are asked out of humility and the person knows you are genuinely interested in what makes them tick and why they made the choices they did. Few things are more impactful than someone who shows a genuine interest in someone else, and this can only be done when humility shows up and says, "Teach me. I want to understand and know what you know."

What Do I Need to Do to Protect Against My Weaknesses?

We all have weaknesses and blind spots. Coach Leaders recognize and seek help for their blind spots, but this doesn't happen without some level of humility. I tend to trust people automatically and give everyone the benefit of the doubt. I have learned some harsh lessons along the way, and now, if the stakes are high, I get input from those I really trust who don't have a blind spot in this area. But early in my career I would often get their input, and then ignore it. So my question is this, Did my arrogance or my humility get me into trouble? Humility is often the fence that protects us from bad decisions.

Arrogance says, "I will never do that."

Humility says, "Just because I never have, doesn't mean I never will."

Humility knows the value of boundaries and accountability partners.

> "Don't ever take a fence down until you
> know the reason it was put up."
>
> —*G. K. Chesterton*

As we grow as business leaders, it is easy to forget about our weaknesses or wrongly believe they are no longer a threat. This is a huge mistake! The more responsibility and authority you have, the greater the imperative to guard against your weaknesses and blind spots.

What Do I Need to Take Full Responsibility and Ownership Of?

Steve Krivda, a Ziglar Legacy speaker and coach, noted, "Most will say they will do anything to accomplish their goals . . . except take responsibility for where they are." Steve has hit on a key factor in the difference between good leaders and great Coach Leaders.

We all have a story. Things happen to us beyond our control and things happen to us because of the choices we make. Every person's story is unique.

Here is the question: Have you taken ownership and responsibility for where you are right now? It takes humility to do this, because all of us have things about ourselves that we are not proud of and we wish were different. In many cases we are not responsible for what happened to us, but we are responsible for how we handle what happens to us. Humility allows us to look at our responses and ask the simple question, How can I handle it better next time?

Arrogance or pride would say, "What do you expect?! What happened to me was terrible and of course I reacted."

Humility would say, "What happened to me was terrible, and I can do better next time and choose to respond differently."

Humility helps you to see the need for taking ownership of your response.

Speak the Truth in Love

As I was studying the virtues that allow us to lead effectively in disruptive times, I remembered a study I had done years ago based on a simple question: As a Christ-follower, what character quality would be the most important for me to develop from God's perspective? Even if you are not a believer, I think you will see the power of this question and the answer. If you like, you can change the question: As a human, what character quality could I develop that would allow me to have the most fulfilling life possible?

In my study I encountered words like *love* and *humility*. These are virtues that God places a high value on, and they are universal, even if you are not a Christian. Then I came across the word *brokenness* in Steven Fry's book *True Freedom*.[7] Brokenness is the ultimate form of humility. In the spiritual context, it doesn't mean you are broken and can't do anything. Instead, it means you understand there is nothing you can do of eternal significance without God's help.

Arrogance says, "I don't need your help."

Humility says, "I need your help."

Brokenness says, "I need God's help."

This is where it gets interesting. The key attribute of a broken person is they speak the truth in love. Truth is never used as a hammer or as a *gotcha* but always as a way to help the receiver discover what is true. It is shared in love for the other's benefit, not used as a weapon to illuminate self-righteousness. When the truth is shared out of arrogance, it usually drives people away from the truth. When it is shared with humility and brokenness, the receiver will often consider it.

Boldness

Brokenness and true humility have a surprising result: boldness. One of the challenges we all have is we want to be liked and, hopefully, respected. We carefully measure our words and our actions with the hope we will be liked and accepted by those around us. This is why people so readily become like the people they spend time with. We want to be accepted so much that instead of doing and saying what is right, we do and say what the group likes. As you can see, picking the wrong group has dire consequences. The wrong group needs the truth spoken in love more than anything, and it takes a humble and broken person to give it to them.

A humble and broken person understands their responsibility is to speak the truth, God's truth, in love. And because it is God's truth, they have no responsibility for how it is received. This deep understanding and application of humility and brokenness means that when you deliver the truth in love, you no longer worry about how the person you are sharing it with will receive it. Their reaction or response to the truth in love is between them and God. What they do with it is up to them and how they feel about you doesn't matter. Your value and your position are secure, and their like or dislike is not about you; it is about their relationship with the truth.

Imagine your team is doing well and all eight team members are exceeding expectations. One day you notice some tension, and it comes to your attention that one of your top performers is gossiping about another team member. The top performer is very well liked, has a lot of influence, is vital to the team's success, and has been very supportive of you.

The mental gymnastics start as you begin to figure out how you are going to address this. The questions start going through your mind: How will he react to me? Will he still like and support me? What will this do to the team? If I don't do anything, will it blow over?

Stop!

Remember: the issue is not between you and the top performer. In fact, it takes some level of arrogance to believe this. The issue is between the top performer and what is true and what is right. The top performer is on the wrong side of what is right, and you, as the Coach Leader, know the truth of this and have the responsibility to share this truth in love with the top performer so he can get back on the right side. The challenge isn't about how he will respond to you; the challenge is how will he respond to the truth? This allows you to be bold, because his acceptance or rejection of your sharing truth is not his accepting or rejecting you, but his accepting or rejecting the truth.

Business Context

Howard Partridge, our exclusive small business coach at Ziglar, puts this approach into a simple question model. Once it has been established and verified by who you are talking with (the top performer) that you are aware of the behavior and he agrees it has happened, you then ask him these questions:

- "Can you tell me what our company mission statement is?" (Everyone on your team should know this by heart. And if the mission statement is too complicated to easily remember, that is something you need to address.) The top performer repeats it.
- "Can you share with me what our company values are?" (A simple, easy-to-remember list of company values is important. These are the truth and what's right in your company.) The top performer repeats it.
- "Help me understand how your behavior [a specific example of the gossip] helps us fulfill our mission and uphold our values."

This approach, delivered from a place of humility (because the standard applies to you as well) with love, now makes the issue between the top performer and the company mission statement and values.

The point of this example is to show you what happens when you step away from arrogance (it's about me) into humility (it's about you and something bigger than me). Humility allows us to do what is right, with love, without worrying about reactions or responses, because when the truth is spoken in love, it is between the individual and the truth.

Humility is not about the worker or the Coach Leader; it is about something bigger than both of them. Humility means you think bigger.

Humility and the Top Performer

Attracting, developing, and retaining top performers is an ongoing challenge that is more difficult than ever before. In the past, many jobs were defined by geography and education. Having the right credentials and living near the office were key to getting the job. Now top performers can live anywhere in the world and work for whomever they choose, and their value is based less on what they already know and more focused on how they can solve new problems in innovative ways.

Almost everyone, and especially top performers, subconsciously ask themselves this question: Is my leader holding me down or lifting me up? Career advancement and achieving personal goals and dreams usually go hand in hand. Top performers are top performers because they have an innate ability to measure their own performance and growth. As part of this evaluation, they ask themselves, Is my leader providing the tools, the support, the atmosphere, the development, the team culture, the collaboration, the innovation, the understanding, the extras I need to do my best work? If the answer is no, what do you think top performers do? They leave. They know their best long-term chance of achieving their goals happens when leadership supports them.

What about the average or good workers? While they may not have taken ownership and full responsibility for their own success, like a top performer does, they still look at their leader and view them either as someone who is helping them advance or as someone who is holding them back. This view is hyperfocused in times of disruption, challenge, and change. If you don't do the things to build and develop your people when things are going smoothly, you aren't going to have the trust to do it when disruption comes.

Humility, Creativity, Culture, Mental Health, and the Question

Imagine you are leading a team of top performers. Some work at the company headquarters and others work remotely. You have a classic blended team in that they are all in the same room together only very rarely. Here is the question for you: Do you think your top performers would prefer to be told what to do, when to do it, and how it should be done; or do you think they would prefer to be asked how they would recommend getting what needs to be done on time and on budget and what help they need?

It turns out everyone would rather be asked than told, especially in their area of expertise. Humility gives your Coach Leader questions more credibility and power because humility means the question is about them, not you. Because humility allows you to focus on their needs, you are better prepared to handle the three big challenges of the blended work team: creativity, culture, and mental health.

Nicholas Bloom is a professor of economics at Stanford University, and he has done extensive research on the impact working remotely has on productivity and performance. "The issues with remote work that always come up are creativity, culture and mental health," he observed.[8]

Coach Leaders recognize the disruption in the form of remote work requires a proactive approach to these concerns. Humility allows the Coach Leader to seek solutions outside of their own experience and ask deeper questions.

- **Creativity:** How can I create an atmosphere of creativity both in one-on-one meetings and team meetings when we are using technology? What questions do I need to ask? What tools do I need to provide? What follow-up methods do I need to implement?
- **Culture:** How do I use our mission statement and values to raise the standard? How do I create engagement and positive interaction? How do I draw on the strengths of each team member?
- **Mental health:** How do I acknowledge that work-life balance can easily get out of kilter? How do I provide support for working-from-home challenges? How do I address the added stress that disruption and change bring to each team member?

What If

What if you are asked a question you don't know the answer to? This is where humility plays a huge part in your success as a Coach Leader. If not knowing the answer to a question creates frustration or resentment, then you are being driven by ego and pride. If, instead, it creates curiosity and a yearning for learning, then humility is where you are coming from. If your focus is on helping the other person, you are in the right place of humility.

Everyone, not just top performers, loves to work where they are valued and recognized. As we move into the future, top performers will have fewer and fewer restrictions on where they can work, because geography and education will mean less and less as converging technologies replace these.

Earlier we quoted Zig Ziglar: "People don't care how much you know, until they know how much you care . . . about them."

Humility allows you to make it about them. Being grateful for your people, their uniqueness and their strengths, allows you to draw out the more capable person inside each of them. Identifying the challenges your people have allows you to ask the questions you need to ask to discover how you can best support them and help them grow. Top performers stay where they are growing and achieving their personal and professional goals.

Humility also means you accept and commit to living up to the mission and values of the organization for which you work. It is impossible to be a truly humble leader without first being humble to a standard higher than yourself. One of the greatest benefits to this is when you are in a position to be bold and address the challenge right away whenever someone on your team has an attitude or behavior that is detrimental to the team and organization. This is done in a coaching conversation, asking the individual a simple question: "Help me understand how this [attitude or behavior] supports the company mission and values." Being humble makes it clear that the problem is between them and the company mission and values.

Humble Coach Leaders are able to serve and support those they lead without feeling threatened or "less than" just because they don't know the answer to a difficult question. Reflect on these three questions as you consider that humility is the only way to grow:

- How can you develop yourself into a humble leader?
- How can you intentionally demonstrate humility as you work with each person on your team and in team meetings?
- What questions can you ask your leadership that will allow you to lead your team more effectively in a humble way?

As the Coach Leader your goal is to automatically create an atmosphere that allows those around you to flourish in every area of their life: at work and at home and with all their relationships. This only happens when you truly become a person who lives out the virtues of kindness, selflessness, respect, and humility. Make it a daily practice to review your schedule of meetings before the day begins, and reflect on how you can approach every interaction with these four virtues as the starting point. Now circle that last sentence if you believe this practice will make you a more effective Coach Leader.

SECTION TWO

HOW DO WE NEED TO BE?

Virtues Focused on Preparing the Team

*Love is patient and kind; love does not envy or boast;
it is not arrogant or rude. It does not insist on its
own way; it is not irritable or resentful; it does not
rejoice at wrongdoing, but rejoices with the truth.
Love bears all things, believes all things, hopes all
things, endures all things.*

Love never ends. . . .

*So now faith, hope, and love abide, these three;
but the greatest of these is love.*

—1 Corinthians 13:4–8, 13

Do your people know you love them? We often think they do. Or we think they know we love them because we judge ourselves by our intentions, not our actions. And yet our people judge us by our actions. If we fly off the handle and are overly negative and critical about them and the work that is being done, we create an atmosphere of distrust and fear that effectively shuts down engagement and collaboration. How we love our people needs to match the love we have for them in our heart.

CHAPTER 7

VIRTUE 5: SELF-CONTROL

Theme: How we face the future.

The best way to face the future is to start by not sabotaging it! Nothing limits future opportunities more than the loss of self-control.

Everything we say should be said with the belief that it will be recorded and revealed.

Self-control starts with your thinking. An effective mindset and life-enhancing beliefs are dependent on self-control. Self-talk, the story you tell yourself, is the foundation for self-control, and when built properly, it allows for effective and impactful communication.

The definition of *self-control*, according to *Oxford Learner's Dictionary*, is "the ability to remain calm and not show your emotions even though you are feeling angry, excited, etc."

Our self-control is demonstrated by our verbal and nonverbal communication, which often are manifestations of the story we tell ourselves.

In times of disruption, challenge, and change, few things are as important as effective communication, and almost nothing can do more damage quicker than the loss of self-control in your communication.

Nothing will reveal your self-control more than when you're attacked in front of your peers and those you lead. As the Coach Leader, when this happens to you, how you either respond or react will greatly affect the trajectory of your career and even your life.

Without self-control you have no real chance of being an effective leader. Lack of self-control has derailed more promising leadership careers than just about any other reason.

In July 2014, I met Mahongo Fumbelo at our Ziglar Legacy Certification (ZLC) program in Dallas. Getting to know her was a delight, and the fact that she came from Darwin, Australia, to participate made her even more interesting. Mahongo is a gifted communicator and very articulate. She is confident and encouraging, and her charisma draws you in and makes you want to listen, learn, and participate. She is the type of leadership expert speaker you look forward to hearing, because you know you will learn something and enjoy it in the process.

The ZLC program is interactive as we are certifying people to teach and train our programs. I had a chance to see Mahongo not only participate in group discussions but also present from the front of the room. I knew right away she was going to be very successful. At the end of the program we have a graduation ceremony, where everyone gets a chance to give a short speech about what the program has meant to them. This is where Mahongo's story took an interesting turn.

Mahongo came to the front of the room, poised and with a big smile, and said, "I almost didn't come here." And then she broke down in tears.

For the next forty-five seconds Mahongo's emotions flowed. They were tears of overcoming, of doing it anyway and in spite of, of relief, of a new beginning. They were the tears of yes! The class was taken aback and concerned, with their hearts leaping out to her. Everyone seemed to think that Mahongo represented the best of all of us; no one had any idea that this was so challenging for her. And then Mahongo told her story.

"I almost didn't come," she said. "Last year, where I worked, I was voted by my peers as the most valuable employee. I loved my job and the people. I was excited about the future, about learning and growing and advancing my career. A little while later our managing director called a team meeting, and we were all brainstorming and discussing how we could meet our goals for the current year. In the meeting I raised my hand and offered my assistance. I said to the group, 'As you know, I have applied for the trainer position, and I have been told that it will be several months before I will know if I am offered the position. However, I want you to know that if there is any skill or knowledge you need to better do your job, just come to me, and I will research it and come back to you with some training that will help you.' After saying this, my boss, in front of my peers, looked at me and pointed at me and said 'Mahongo, you will never be a trainer at this company. You don't have the personality or the skills to train, so you can just forget about that position.'"

She paused. The whole room was completely silent in disbelief. I knew Mahongo was one of the best participants in the program. When I thought about her boss, I asked myself, *Who does that, and especially to her?*

"I didn't know what to do," Mahongo resumed. "Part of me wanted to storm out of the room, make a scene, quit on the spot. Instead, I sat down, silent and expressionless, and I counted the minutes until the meeting was over. As I was walking back to my office, I started thinking about the resignation letter I would write and how I would blast the boss in my exit interview. And then I started thinking about my dream, my passion to be a speaker, trainer, and coach. Was my boss right? It shook me to the core."

Self-control.

"I went to my office," she said, "closed the door, and started to think and to pray. I decided to wait until I cooled off to say anything to my company. I had to decide who I would believe and how I would cast my vote. Would I give up and cower in the corner, controlled by someone who didn't even know me, or would I stand up and choose to step into my dream, even if it was on my own? I chose to believe what God says about me, what I say about me, rather than what anyone else who doesn't know my heart says about me."

"That night," she continued, "as I was struggling with all of this, I remembered a message I had seen from Ziglar about becoming a Ziglar speaker and trainer. I reached out right away. And here I am. This is me."

At this point the entire graduating class was on their feet and applauding as they wiped away tears of support, care, love, and joy for Mahongo. No one, other than Mahongo, was crying more than I was.

One year later, in August 2015, I had the opportunity to do a live event with Mahongo in Darwin, on her stage for her customers. Needless to say, I wasn't the most effective communicator in the room. Mahongo was.

Mahongo has gone on to create a very successful speaking, training, and coaching business, and she has been recognized in Australia through Toastmasters as one of the top speakers in the country. She now is the Coach Leader to so many other Coach Leaders, equipping them through her speaking, training, coaching, and consulting to lead their people. How did this happen? I believe her immense self-control allowed her to rise above the pressure and the unfairness of the situation. The irony is her self-control gave her a bigger stage than she could even imagine.

As if this story isn't already good enough, it gets even better. In October 2018 I received the following email from Mahongo:

I just wanted to share something interesting with you. You're the first person I am telling after my family as you've been a part of my journey and now my success. The employer who said they couldn't give me the promotion as training facilitator because I didn't have the right personality called me last week to ask me to deliver training for their clients as well as their leadership team. They told me that they have struggled to find any good trainers and they came across my website and they loved what they saw. The lady who called me said she remembered me as one of their most talented employees they had.

I am so grateful for what you and the rest of the Ziglar family did for me as I have experienced so many blessings and successes that I know I could never have accomplished without your encouragement. While I have mixed blessings about working with my former employer as an external consultant, I know for sure that God is reassuring me of His plans for my life and perhaps soon I'll achieve my wildest dream of speaking to an audience of 5000 in the US!

I thought I would just share this with my favorite family in the US.

Self-control starts with mindset and belief. Would Mahongo's story be different if she had lost her self-control and reacted by blowing up at the leader who attacked her in front of her peers? Absolutely! Would her story be different if she had chosen to believe her boss rather than what she believed about herself? Most certainly.

Three Keys to Mastering Self-Control When You Are Communicating Under Stress

1. Know what you believe and your purpose for being in that situation.

Mahongo believed she was on a journey to becoming an effective speaker, trainer, and coach and that she could best do that by helping others along the way as she developed her skills. Her offer to help made the boss's attack even more of a blindside. The clarity and depth of her belief allowed her to respond rather than react. Her mindset was focused.

What do you believe?

What is the higher purpose you are fulfilling by communicating well under pressure?

2. Ask, would a secure person do that?

Whenever I am attacked, I ask myself, Would a secure person do that? The attack could be an email, on social media, in a face-to-face conversation, in a team meeting, or in front of a group. Attacks are never appropriate, especially in front of others, and most especially if the attacker has more positional power than you. The fact is a secure person would not do that. Because I know this, I immediately understand that this is an insecure person. This thought immediately changes the way I view my attacker and lowers my emotional state from fighting back at them to concern for them. Why? Because when someone communicates from insecurity, I know I am not the one who has a problem, but they do.

Would a secure person say or do that?

Why are they insecure?

3. Recall the mental model for self-control in communicating.

I was speaking for my friend John Rouse in Wichita, Kansas. The morning leading up to the presentation had more than a few distractions, and it seemed all the little things that could go wrong were going wrong. There was also some discord I would learn more about later that seemed to make the atmosphere tense. The good news was the room was full and excitement was building. Then, just before I was to speak, an elderly woman fell in the middle of the aisle, right in front of the podium. She was not hurt or in obvious pain, but it was decided to call the paramedics to check her out and allow them to lift her off the floor. This delayed the start of the program by twenty-five minutes, but it didn't push back when I had to finish.

John came to me, concerned about this setback. I told him, "Everything is going to be okay. When these types of things go on, you know that something big and life-changing is about to happen. I am not here to give a set talk. I am here to meet the needs in the room."

The Story You Tell Yourself

We have a choice when it comes to the story we tell ourselves. I work with leaders who admit they doubt themselves, which is illustrated by the story they tell themselves. When I ask what is running through their mind before an important conversation or presentation, they say things such as:

- Why would they listen to me? I am young, brand new. I have issues. I'm unsure.
- I'm not a good presenter.
- I'm in over my head.
- No matter what I say, it won't make a difference.
- I am not _____ enough.

I tell them to make the story you tell yourself *powerful*.
Try this approach:

- I am excited to meet/speak/present today because I believe _____ and my purpose is _____.

- I know the needs of the individual/group are _____ and the goal of the meeting is _____.
- Things beyond my control are likely to happen and I may even be challenged. This is fantastic, because I am here to serve the people and meet their needs as we move toward our purpose and goals.
- If I am attacked, then I know I am dealing with an insecure person and will respond accordingly.

The following is a classic example of self-control and powerful communication from Thomas Jody, a Ziglar Legacy Certified speaker.

Many years ago, as a service writer in an auto dealership, I dealt with a man who, after having his car in for service the previous day, came roaring through the open garage door and slammed on the brakes. He leaped out of the car and threw his sizable wad of keys at me. Fortunately, they landed short and slid down the long service desk and over the end. He began to scream about a particular problem with his car that we hadn't fixed but we had charged him for. He got in my face. At that point, he was loud enough that several of the mechanics in the shop stopped working and came out of their work areas. I calmly asked him to show me the problem, which he did. I asked him to wait a moment while I retrieved his keys. I brought the keys back to him and told him I felt that he had a legitimate complaint. But I also told him we were not going to deal with anything at all until we could deal with it on a civil basis. I asked him to get back in his car and come back the next day, after he had cooled off, and we would take care of the problem at no additional charge. He tried to complain again, and I repeated that we would never respond to an outburst like his today or any day, and he should come back tomorrow with a different attitude. He did.

We fixed his car. Everyone was happy, and he became a regular and more pleasant service customer. His lesson was my lesson. We both learned that we have a choice.

What I love about this story is it highlights the reality that someone is always watching how you respond to a challenging situation. Imagine you're one of the mechanics witnessing how Thomas handled the situation. What would you think of him? Challenging circumstances and times have a way of revealing who you really are. The only good approach is to prepare in advance for the way you will handle the challenge!

Time to Reflect

Put yourself in the place of either Mahongo or Thomas. Knowing how you currently behave, how would you have likely handled their situations? What would you have done differently? Now think about situations you have faced in the past when you were attacked unfairly. How did you handle it? Now take a moment and think about a potential attack you could face in the future and how you, as a Coach Leader, would handle it.

Self-control is calm under pressure and possesses an ability to respond rather than react. As a Coach Leader, few things will undermine your ability to lead quicker than the loss of self-control, and few things will gain respect faster than a demonstration of self-control in the most unfair and difficult situations. Take some time now to develop self-control before you need it, because extreme, pressure-filled situations reveal character more than they create character, and self-control is the shield that protects your leadership influence.

- How can you prepare yourself in advance to keep your cool . and demonstrate self-control when challenges come?
- How can you demonstrate leadership and self-control in your communication with your team when you are under pressure?
- How can you lead when you know they are going through difficult times? What types of communication would support them?

Gentleness, self-control; against such things there is no law. (Galatians 5:23)

A man without self-control is like a city broken into and left without walls. (Proverbs 25:28)

For God gave us a spirit not of fear but of power and love and self-control. (2 Timothy 1:7)

CHAPTER 8

VIRTUE 6: POSITIVITY

Theme: A positive attitude outperforms a negative attitude every time.

"You win some, you learn some."
—JASON MAREZ

"I am so positive I would go after Moby Dick in a rowboat and take the tartar sauce with me!"
—ZIG ZIGLAR

I was raised to be positive. My childhood was marked by opportunities to be positive, regardless of what was happening. I remember, as a seventh grader, craving sleep on a Sunday morning after staying up late on Saturday night. Dad came in to wake me at 7:00 a.m. to get ready for church.

Rubbing the sleep from my eyes, I asked, "Do I have to go to church?"

He looked at me and smiled. "No, son, you *get* to go to church."

At an early age I understood a profound lesson: whatever happened to me or whatever I had or needed to do, I had a choice as to how I viewed it. I learned that you can be positive about things you don't even like!

I love the story Chris Patterson told about his first meeting with Zig Ziglar. Chris was an up-and-coming manager with The Q Athletic Club. The Q was an upscale workout facility, and Chris had demonstrated an ability to lead and develop a successful and profitable club. Because of this, he was transferred to Texas to take over the West Plano Q and to improve profitability and sales. When Chris arrived, the club was ranked near the bottom of the seventeen other locations in the United States. Immediately he began teaching his staff the Ziglar sales and personal development programs that had made him and his previous clubs so successful, and the location was soon ranked number one in the entire country.

After several months of developing his team and seeing improvement in all areas, one of his team members said to him, "There's someone at the front desk that you should give the club tour to."

Chris responded, "I've trained you guys to do the tours and you're doing fantastic. Why would you want me to do the tour?"

His team member handed him the prospect's driver's license. It was Zig Ziglar's. The team knew that Zig Ziglar was Chris's hero!

Chris's heart sank when he realized this wasn't a joke and his real-life hero was in the building. As he gave the tour, he was careful to make sure he didn't reveal that he knew my dad and that he was a huge fan. The tour went well, and it was time for Chris to have the sales conversation with Zig. He explained the options and started using sales questions and closes he learned from listening to all Zig Ziglar's material.

Suddenly, Zig had a wry smile on his face. "You know who I am, don't you?"

Chris couldn't help it. "Yes sir, and I'm a *huge* fan, and I'm so glad you're going to be a part of the Q. Are you ready to get started?"

Needless to say, Zig signed up on the spot.

On the way out, Zig told Chris, "I need someone to personally train me. Who do you recommend?"

Chris smiled. "Mr. Ziglar, I will make you a deal. I will be your physical trainer if you will agree to be my mental coach while I'm training you. Does that sound good to you?"

"That sounds great, Chris. What time tomorrow do we start?"

Chris couldn't believe it! Not only had he sold his hero a membership to the Q, but he was also going to be his trainer and be mentored by him.

The next day Zig arrived and they began the initial workout. The first exercise was a biceps exercise called the Preacher Curl on a piece of equipment. Zig sat down and began doing curls before Chris could adjust the weight. Chris had told him the goal was ten reps, and it became apparent after the third rep that there was too much weight on the machine.

"Mr. Ziglar, hold on a second and let me lower the weight."

Zig just smiled and kept on lifting. After three more reps, the veins started popping out on his forehead. Chris thought, *Oh, no! Zig is going to have a heart attack, and the headline in tomorrow's paper is going to be "Young Punk Trainer Kills Legendary Speaker and Author Zig Ziglar on His Very First Workout!"*

Zig was really struggling, and Chris said, "Mr. Ziglar, stop lifting and let me adjust the weight."

Instead of stopping, a determined look came over Zig's face as he struggled to get reps eight, nine, and ten completed.

"That's great, Mr. Ziglar! You can stop now. You've hit ten."

But Zig kept on lifting. Eleven, twelve, and finally thirteen reps.

As Zig put the weights down, he looked Chris in the eye and said, "You don't have to like everything you do."

I love this story because it illustrates the foundation of what being positive means, namely, you don't have to like everything you do, because you understand you have a goal and a purpose worth achieving. Zig's goal and purpose was to be the most effective speaker, author, husband, and father possible. Because of this, he knew that good health was essential to his goals. This understanding allowed him to be positive and have the right attitude, even when doing the necessary things he didn't like.

Positively Contagious

Are you positively contagious when you are around your family, your friends, and your coworkers? Does your presence alone create energy and hopefulness around those you work with and lead? Have you ever been around someone who lifted the spirits in the room just by their attitude? Do you believe that being positively contagious would help you and your team achieve their goals and objectives more easily, even in times of disruption?

Read the above paragraph again. Answering yes to the questions are essential to your success as a Coach Leader. Being positive in times of disruption, challenge, and change is not an option if you want to be an effective Coach Leader!

Unfortunately, people often have the wrong understanding of what being positive means. Being positive is not a fake, everything's okay, don't worry about the facts, blind faith that ignores what is really going on. Being positive means that no matter what's going on, you understand you have a choice of how you are going to respond to the situation. You know it is not only what you do but how you do it that inspires and encourages your team. Let's dig into what being positive really means.

The word *positive* has one of the longest and most extensive definitions in *Merriam-Webster's Dictionary*. This is because *positive* is used in so many different ways. For you to be positive as a Coach Leader, you need to understand exactly what you need to develop in yourself and demonstrate by example to those around you.

Traits of the Positive Coach Leader: Moving from Theory to Application

The positive Coach Leader is *confident* and fully assured. Coach Leaders are confident they can ask the right questions that will allow them to discover the best way forward. Many people wrongly assume this confidence is fake bluster and prefer to take the safe route of painting an overly negative picture so they don't look bad if the results don't come. The reality is the safe and negative route limits and restricts the available positive outcomes. After all, if it is hopeless and terrible, why spend time trying to solve an unsolvable problem?

Being confident doesn't mean you already have the answers. It simply means you know a process and have built strong relationships with those who either can provide the solutions or connect you with those who can. This confidence is especially essential when significant challenges arise. Coach Leaders who have this confidence are able to be vulnerable, transparent, and confident at the same time, because it is not necessary they have the answer; they know how to find the answer.

Focus on What You Can Do

Being positive means circumstances do not determine the emotional state and response of Coach Leaders. In fact, Coach Leaders relish challenge and change, because changing circumstances highlight their strengths and advantages. The positive mindset views disruption simply as an opportunity to grow, adapt, and serve others in their time of need.

The positive Coach Leader has an incredible amount of grit, which is defined by Angela Duckworth in the book *Grit*,[9] as the ability to continue to get up even when knocked down over and over again. The positive Coach Leader looks at every challenge, every disruption, every change as an opportunity to grow, to learn, and to get up again. Few things set a more powerful example than how a leader handles adversity.

Being positive also means that you are *real*. When challenges and problems come, the Coach Leader clearly identifies the problems and challenges. This includes carefully considering the impact the problems will have and the resources and people necessary to overcome the problems. Illuminating the problems and challenges allows everyone on the team to clearly grasp what needs to be done.

Coach Leaders understand that being positive means they have to take action toward their goal on a consistent basis and not focus on maintaining the status quo. Coach Leaders never get trapped in a comfort zone, because they know there is no such thing. As Ziglar Legacy speaker Carey Lowe observed, "People, teams, and businesses are either growing or dying. There is no such thing as 'the comfort zone' where it is okay to coast." Being positive means taking positive action toward your purpose and goal.

Positive Coach Leaders focus on what they can do, not on what they can't do. In their relationships with others this is characterized by affirmation and inclusion rather than by negation or disengagement. The can-do attitude is lived out in emails, phone conversations, team meetings, and Zoom calls. Coach Leaders phrase their questions to their teams in positive, action-oriented ways.

A Coach Leader identifies positive sources of inspiration, motivation, and growth and will constantly invest time with them. Not only do Coach Leaders do this for themselves, but they also give their team a high standard and the resources they can move toward that will encourage and develop them in their own growth toward their own goals.

Being positive means you have a favorable effect on those you work with. One of the best ways to determine your impact on your team is to have them fill out an anonymous questionnaire on your impact on their performance. A great question is, After working directly with your leader, do you feel hopeful, inspired, and equipped to take on the challenges and disruptions that are happening in your work situation? Their answers will give you great insight into how your leadership is being perceived and received.

Being Positive Is Smart!

"A positive attitude won't let you do anything, but it will let you do everything better than a negative attitude will."

—Zig Ziglar

Often the so-called educated and enlightened will say it's practical and beneficial to be skeptical and even negative about situations. They use this as justification for their sour attitudes and habitually demanding and demeaning communication styles. But is this really the smart and practical way to approach disruption, challenge, and change?

Imagine you are in your office, planning for the coming year. You have just reviewed all the results from the previous year. You've done an inventory of your key accounts, projects, and strategies with an eye toward improvement and growth. Plus you have implemented a comprehensive development plan for your people.

Suddenly, the CEO comes in and says your organization has lost its funding and your top account has left to go with your number-one competitor. Twenty minutes later your top salesperson resigns, and you realize all your plans now need to be reworked.

As you start to dig into the new planning, a team member tells you the team is very concerned about the CEO's news that, like a tsunami, is making its way through the company. You decide to call an all-hands-on-deck meeting to bring everyone up to speed. Which of the following approaches do you think will get the best results?

Approach 1:

Thank you, everyone, for coming to this meeting. You have already heard about the situation. Cash flow is going to be tight because we have lost our funding, and on top of that, our largest account has gone to a competitor, and our top salesperson who developed that account and several others has also left for another opportunity.

I want you to know this is devastating for me as your leader and for our company. I am not sure how we are going to get through this, and, in fact, this place will most likely look vastly different in just a short amount of time. If you have been thinking about leaving, go ahead and turn in your resignation today. There are going to be many difficult situations in the coming weeks and many difficult decisions that I will have to make. Unfortunately, I have been through this before, and it is not easy or fun, and many lives will be changed in a negative way. I need to take some time for myself to sort this out, and I would encourage you to do the same. Thank you for your understanding. Now go back to work.

Approach 2:

Thank you, everyone, for coming to this meeting. You have already heard about the situation. Cash flow is going to be tight because we have lost our funding, and on top of that, our largest account has gone to our competitor, and our top salesperson who developed that account and several others has also left for another opportunity.

These are the facts as we know them right now, and I want you to be aware of them. However, there is something more important than the facts, and that is the people you are surrounded by right now. I was just reviewing last year's accomplishments and all the things we have overcome as a team, and I am grateful that we are going to face this challenge together. I can guarantee you there will be some challenging times ahead, but they will also be filled with innovation, creativity, and the knowledge that there is nothing more satisfying than overcoming a difficult challenge with people you love and care about. The mission and values of our company haven't changed, and the need for our products and services is greater than ever. I would like to spend the rest of our time today focusing on and remembering the challenges and the victories we've had together that have brought us here, and then we will start creating an action list of what we can do to make this day legendary in all the right ways for our business.

Being Positive Means You Have a Plan

The second approach is the obvious way to address massive change and disruption. This approach recognizes the facts, but also, more importantly, recognizes how we respond to the facts will determine the results we get.

The Halftime Speech

Have you ever wondered what goes on at halftime when a coach is addressing his team when they're down by three touchdowns? Do you think the coach complains about the officiating, about the injuries, about everything that is so unfair? Or do you think the coach has a plan as to what to say and how to say it before the game even starts, in case there is a need for an inspiring and moving halftime speech?

What is your plan when your team is behind at halftime? Have you even thought about it? One thing we know for sure is that, if you are a Coach Leader for long enough, you will be called on to lead your team when things don't look good and the score is not in your favor. The following is a step-by-step plan you can tailor for when this situation arises in your business.

1. Be positive. Everyone is looking to you for leadership in this situation. You can be intense, passionate, or concerned, but most of all you must be positive. Your team should know your vision and your expectations before this situation ever arises. This way, when the setbacks and the disruptions come, you can let them know with confidence that they are still going to accomplish the mission and the vision that is before them. Your body language and your voice inflection confirm the mission has not changed and you believe the people in the room are up to the task of overcoming the challenges confronting them.

2. Be prepared. Just as coaches have to be prepared for halftime, you and your team have to know and believe you have already done what's necessary to prepare for this situation. Preparation simply means you have done everything possible ahead of time so you can accomplish your business goals regardless of what happens. When disruption and change occur, and you realize you need to adjust to new circumstances, prior preparation gives you confidence that you can learn, understand, grow, and prepare again.

3. Take a timeout for gratitude. Being a positive Coach Leader means you understand that sometimes you have to take time out for gratitude. Recognizing that your team needs an attitude shift is part of being an effective leader. One of the best ways to change a negative mindset for an individual or a group is to have them list what they are grateful for. It is very difficult to be both grateful and negative at the same time. The best way to do this is to start the discussion by explaining what you are grateful for. You can let everyone know you are grateful you have a team of people who have overcome similar challenges in the past. You can let them know you are grateful you are their leader and that your team has a proven ability to adapt and grow. Pointing out specific character traits that the people on your team have and how they have helped in the past and how they are perfect for this situation will quickly inspire a can-do attitude. Once you establish what it means to take a timeout for gratitude, you can call on someone else on the team to express what they are grateful for. Depending on the situation, you can make this voluntary or you can let everyone know you will call on all of them to participate. Gratitude is the healthiest of all human emotions, and now is the time you and your team need this more than ever.

4. Create a victory list. Now that gratitude is flowing and people are moving into what they can do, it's time to create a victory list. One of the habits of high-performing positive Coach Leaders is they keep track of the victories each of their people have had. This list can include victories you have shared with them or victories they experienced before they came to the team. A great way to start this conversation is to ask a specific question to a team member, such as "Tell me about the time you had the _____ challenge and what you did to overcome it." You can even ask more detailed questions, such as, "I know when that challenge came up, you were concerned whether we would be able to solve it, and we did. What were you worried about and how did you overcome it?" Now, as the leader, it is a great time to get the team engaged in the victory list topper game, namely, simply asking someone what challenge or difficulty they have overcome in their past. Feel free to prompt them, based on your relationship and knowledge of their past. Creating a victory list reassures the team that they have done it before and they can do it again. Now the team is ready to get into problem-solving.

5. Clarify the problem. The most important part of problem-solving is getting crystal-clear clarity on what the problem is and the team's responsibility for fixing it. This is essential in times of disruption and change, because there are problems that arise, such as a pandemic, that the team has no ability to fix. If the team or an individual has no ability to fix the problem, then the problem needs to be accepted as a fact, and the focus needs to move on to problems the individual or team can fix. A simple example of this is that when the pandemic happened, many businesses were forced to work from home. The leaders of those businesses couldn't fix the pandemic, but they could do many things to make working from home more effective.

6. Focus on the solution. In the process of clarifying the problem, it often becomes clear there are several different problems that need to be solved. Each of these problems should be handled separately. Now we can get specific with the team's input or the individuals concerned, as not everyone on the team will work on every problem. Following are three great questions to ask:

- What are the major obstacles and mountains to climb to solve this problem?

- What are the skills or knowledge required to solve this problem?
- Who are the individuals, groups, or outside resources to work with to solve this problem?

7. Plan the solution. Now is the time to create a plan with the team's participation on how the problem will be solved. Depending on the type of problem and the amount of time needed to create the plan, this process can be either very detailed or limited to the most important bullet points, with the details being filled in later. The critical aspect of this activity is to identify the actions that can be taken immediately.

8. Ownership and timeline. Once the plan or the outline for the plan has been created, each actionable item needs to be assigned a priority and a timeline for when it will be completed.

9. Recap. It is time for you to recap what has just occurred. You have just demonstrated the disruption, challenge, or problem can be approached from a proactive and positive perspective by building confidence in the team, clarifying the problem, outlining the solutions, creating a plan, and assigning priorities, ownership, and timelines. Being positive throughout this process allows the team to move from fearful inaction to positive action as fast as possible.

> ## "Culture eats strategy for breakfast."
>
> *—Peter Drucker*

Being positive is key to establishing the right culture, living out your values, and creating a high performing environment. As discussed in chapter 2, atmosphere is the combination of culture, values, and environment. Let's take a detailed look at how being positive as a Coach Leader has a huge impact on the atmosphere you create.

Start with your mission statement. For the purpose of illustration, we will use the following real estate brokerage company mission state-ment as an example.

> **Mission:** To provide the most phenomenal home-buying experience possible.
>
> **Question:** Is it possible to provide a phenomenal home-buying experience with a bad attitude? Of course not.

Being positive as a Coach Leader means you are constantly evalu-ating your culture in relationship to the mission of your team and your company. A positive culture is simply the fruit of being an attentive and positive leader. Strategy is important to your team success; how-ever, the effective execution of the strategy depends on the culture of the team.

Write down your company's (or your team's) mission statement.

List three reasons that being positive allows you to fulfill that mis-sion more effectively, and follow that with three reasons as to why being negative will hurt your ability to fulfill the mission.

Next, list your company values.

Now ask yourself how important it is, on a scale of one to ten, to be positive versus being negative to live out and be an example of these values.

Eye-Opening

It is amazing how eye-opening it is to look at being positive in the light of accomplishing our most important objectives. As the world continues to change and more disruption comes, it will become even more important for the Coach Leader to maintain a positive approach in the business world. As more and more people work from home, and as technology disrupts the way business has been done in the past, a positive mindset will be central to embracing these changes.

Being positive is essential to maximizing people, purposes, and performances. Being positive allows you to influence your team, your prospects, your customers, and your vendors in a way that attracts them and draws out the best in them. Being positive helps you to connect the company's purpose with the purpose each team member has in their own life. Being positive creates the atmosphere that allows for maximum performance.

- How can you create a positive attitude in yourself?
- How can you lead your team and help them develop a positive attitude?
- How can you support and create a positive attitude in your leaders?

CHAPTER 9

VIRTUE 7: LOOKING FOR THE BEST

Theme: Expect the best. Prepare for the worst. Maximize what comes.

Looking for the best in people in change and in opportunities gives fuel, hope, and the energy to keep moving forward.

"We create the future we see."

—Tom Ziglar

What future do you see? Looking for the best is one of the most distinguishing attributes of a great Coach Leader. When you look into the future, what do you envision?

- A better life for you and your family?
- Advancing in your career?
- Achieving your goals and dreams?
- Building a successful team?

- Being a respected life-changing leader?

When you look into the future of the people you're leading, what do you envision?

- Success in their personal and professional lives?
- Growth and development in their skills and attitude?
- The ability to handle disruption, challenge, and change?
- Each of them becoming a leader, a valued and trustworthy team member, even a friend you can count on?

Go Ahead and Say What You Want

As you look into the future, take a few moments now to say what you want regarding your own business leadership capacity, the growth and results you will obtain, and the type of people you will work with and grow with to achieve these goals. Once this becomes crystal clear in your mind, you can begin to create the future that you see.

When you understand and believe you can create the future that you see, it dramatically changes your thinking. Imagine an incredible challenge and disruption in front of you. Your view of the future will determine the way you think about and take action regarding this challenge and disruption. If you are excited and hopeful for the future, your thinking will remain positive regarding the challenge, and you will view it as one more thing to overcome on the way to your goal. If your view of the future is negative and hopeless, the new setback or challenge is just another reason to give up and go home.

Creating the future you want depends on how you see the future. How you see the future determines your thinking, and your thinking determines your performance.

Gold Rush

I love the TV series *Gold Rush*. There is something about risking everything and putting yourself in extreme conditions, risking life and limb to discover gold. The gold could be under layers of soil, rock, and ice or it could be at the bottom of a raging river or an arctic sea. And yet, because gold is so valuable, the gold miners go in, focused on the gold, not the dirt, the frigid water, or the raging storms.

Looking for the best means you are looking for the gold, not the dirt.

Looking for the best doesn't mean you are unrealistic or overly positive with your outlook. It means you take ownership of your thinking and prepare in advance for anything that can disrupt what you want to accomplish. Zig Ziglar's quote, "Expect the best. Prepare for the worst. Maximize what comes" is a great way to view this concept.

Expect the best: This is 100 percent about your mindset and beliefs. Focus on what you can do. Focus on solutions. Make sure to choose your input wisely. Use the extra time on your hands to develop yourself and your business/career. There is no downside to this, and science agrees. A positive mindset has great health benefits. A fear-driven, negative mindset hurts your immune system and causes other physical illnesses. Expecting the best means you have clearly identified the future you want to create, and you are aligning your mindset and beliefs to give you the best chance of creating this future. As a Coach Leader, it also means you expect the best from everyone on your team. Great Coach Leaders understand that sometimes they have to transfer their confidence and belief to those they lead before their people will believe in themselves. This makes it essential for you, the Coach Leader, to continually work on your own mindset and belief.

Prepare for the worst: Yes, absolutely make sure your storehouse is full and you have reserves in place. Absolutely use wisdom in your daily life and social interactions. And while you are preparing, tell your mind that you get to do now all the things you have been putting off. Focus on what you can do, not what you can't do. Just as in *Gold Rush*, when the miners prepare for harsh weather and life-threatening circumstances in advance, you need to prepare in advance for when disruption and change come. Your team will not be surprised when the challenge comes, and neither will you. The only question will be, Have you prepared as best you can for the challenge?

Maximize what comes: No one knows what tomorrow or next week or next month has in store for us. If your mindset is right, if you are focused on serving others, if you are intentional about growing yourself, then you will be perfectly positioned to make a difference in this world, and that will allow you to have the biggest impact possible. Focus on serving others and solving problems. The greatest benefit of disruption is that it exposes new problems or reveals overlooked existing problems. As a Coach Leader focused on a growth mindset, you will be in your element, because instead of seeing problems, you will see opportunities.

A Simple Example

Let's say everything is going well with your team. Your projects and revenue goals are ahead of schedule and the future looks bright. Everyone on the team has hit their stride, and then you learn that your top performer is leaving for another opportunity. Everything you had just been reflecting on is now up in the air. What do you do? Do you have a pity party, lower your expectations, and realize you have to take on a lot of extra work? Or do you celebrate your top performer getting a dream job and start to get excited about developing the remaining people on your team to grow into the position your top performer is leaving? Either way your problem is the *same*. Which mindset and attitude do you think will get the best result?

Creating Alignment When Disruption Comes

Looking for the best is not only a virtue but also a mindset that is incredibly valuable in creating alignment, especially when disruption and challenges occur with those you are leading. As a Coach Leader, when you work with people long enough, it is only a matter of time before performance and attitudes will need to be addressed. Even top performers will experience rough patches from time to time, and addressing these proactively from the perspective of looking for the best with a growth mindset allows you to maintain your momentum and encourage and develop your people to the next level.

> "Don't wish it were easier, wish you were better."
>
> *—Jim Rohn*

Jim Rohn's observation is perfect to share with someone you are coaching to the next level. Pointing out that their performance is not up to speed or that a relationship is not positive does little good, unless there is a specific plan on how the person can get better. Looking for the best allows you to turn challenges into growth opportunities to become better.

The following are fourteen ways you can connect with people who are causing a disruption or challenge from a positive perspective that will transform temporary challenges into the fuel that elevates someone to the next level of growth. Continuously focusing on the best and helping your team members identify what the best is creates alignment between their personal and professional goals and the mission of your business.

1. Identify. When addressing a challenge with an individual on your team, you must clearly identify what the challenge is, with the goal being that the person grows and overcomes the challenge. Growth is essential, because this prevents the same challenge from reoccurring. In order for growth to occur, the person you are coaching must learn and implement something new. Individuals are far more likely to take your advice and direction if they can identify with you. Think about a similar situation in your past when you had a challenge to overcome, someone advised you on how to overcome it, you took that advice, and the problem was solved. Being vulnerable in this conversation by owning your role in a past problem and the impact it had on your life, and then sharing the journey of overcoming it, will let your team member know that everyone goes through growing pains. Daniel Coyle revealed in his book *The Talent Code*[10] that those who identify with the person giving advice are 30 percent more likely to try the advice long enough to get a result. This approach also clearly defines that the problem is the problem, and the person can own, grow, and learn to solve the problem. Everyone experiences the challenge of growing through situations such as this.

2. Remember how much you have grown. As you look for the best in the person you are coaching, reflect on how much you have grown. List areas in your personal and professional life where you have had significant growth. Spend some time remembering how awkward you felt when you messed up, thinking you were doing the right thing only to realize that you don't know what you don't know. Looking at how much you have grown will confirm that others can grow as well and will allow you to better see their growth potential rather than the circumstances of the problem you're in.

3. Forgive others as you would like to be forgiven. Take a moment to imagine what the person you are coaching is feeling and thinking. Is the individual self-conscious, scared, uncomfortable, defensive, feeling attacked, or completely unaware? Is the person concerned about the relationship with you as the team leader as well as with the others on the team? Does the individual feel strongly about being right or upset that the issue has arisen and feeling the weight of being blamed unfairly? As you gain clarity on how your team member is feeling regarding this challenge and the growth that will need to occur in order to bring them back into alignment with the team and the company values and mission, ask yourself, How would I like to be treated and even forgiven if I were in this situation? When we understand how we would like to be treated in a situation, it allows us to treat better someone else in that situation.

4. Reflect. Take some time, slow down. Look at the big picture and reflect on how much the person has grown, learned, and contributed to the success of the team. Ask yourself how this disruption and challenge the person has contributed to are impacting the team. Is it a minor disruption that, with acknowledgment, growth, and correction, can bring alignment with very little impact to the team's performance? Or is it a significant disruption that will take weeks or even months of concerted effort to bring about the repair and the growth necessary to restore alignment? Recognizing the significance of the situation will allow you to create the right framework as you co-create the necessary growth plan.

5. Start by looking for the good. Now that you have the foundation set regarding the person in the situation, start by looking for the good as you plan your course of action. Ask yourself "good finder" questions, such as, How much more valuable to the team will this person be when they overcome this? How will the way you handle this situation positively impact others on the team? What attitudes and skills will you need to grow in your own leadership to handle this situation more effectively and prevent future situations similar to this from occurring? Coach Leaders understand that these "good finder" questions will show you the wisdom of handling this with your full attention and in the proper way, displaying all ten virtues we are covering in this book.

6. Intentions and motives. As you begin the coaching conversation with your team member, don't assume anything. Get clarity not only on the facts of the situation but also on their intentions and motivations behind what they did with simple and direct questions, such as, "Why did you make this decision?" "What led you to have this conversation with so-and-so?" "Why did you decide to do this when it was already decided we would do something else?" As you dig into these types of questions, it's always a good strategy to follow up a question with another question, especially, "Can you tell me more about that?" Each of the ways covered thus far are focused on understanding the situation and letting the person you are coaching know you care about their perspective and want their input as you create the growth plan to overcome the situation.

7. Sum it up and get agreement. Starting with the facts and getting agreement on them is the best place to begin building a personal development and growth plan to overcome a problem. When you have the initial meeting with your team member, and you discuss the situation at hand and understand their position, then clearly sum up the facts. Start by saying, "Let me repeat back to you what we've covered and what we need to do next. Is that okay?" It's always good to get agreement, because your team member might want to share more before you go on. After you have recapped the conversation, ask, "Does that sum it up accurately or do we need to add anything to this or discuss anything else?" Again, this gives the team member an opportunity to shed additional light on the situation. Once they have said everything, ask, "Is it okay if we work together on a personal development and growth plan to address the situation and make sure you know how to handle it correctly the next time it comes up?" Make sure to get agreement on this next step and get confirmation that they are good with it. When they say yes, make it clear to them that you are excited about their taking ownership in their own growth, because this is the key to advancing in every area of life.

8. Skill. When you are working with someone to overcome a challenge or to develop them in a way that makes them more effective in their role, a great place to start is to identify the skills they bring to the work environment. The skills they currently possess will allow you to align the work more effectively when they are assigned per their current capabilities. Next, you will want to identify the skills they will need to develop to grow in effectiveness in their position. Coach Leaders understand that co-creation in this process with the person they are working with is essential, and this conversation is extremely helpful for understanding the long-term goals and objectives of the person they are working with. When this person shares with you their goals and aspirations, you can then work with them to identify the skills they need to cultivate to achieve those goals. In the case of team members falling short in their performance, it is important to identify the skills needed to perform and then determine if they have already developed those skills. In almost every case, the skills they lack that led to poor performance are the skills they need to acquire to achieve their goals and aspirations for the future. In the development and growth plan, identify the skills that are needed and devise a specific plan of action and timetables for the team member to learn and develop these desired skills.

9. Attitude. Attitude is simply the outward reflection of our character qualities, and our character qualities are a reflection of our habits. A sour, negative, grumpy attitude is a reflection of someone's character, but these negative attitudes are also a reflection of that person's maturity. Frustrations, setbacks, and unplanned changes will all reveal a person's maturity and character through the attitudes they exhibit.

And attitudes are very contagious; they will either lift up or destroy a team's morale and work ethic. When a challenge or disruption is created by a team member's attitude, it is sometimes difficult to look for the best. The best way to do this is to meet with the negative team member privately and take them through a simple process. Start by asking what's going on and why their attitude is negative. Once they've had a chance to explain or even deny their attitude, you can move to the next step, which is to share what you and the other team members have observed about their attitude. In this conversation it's very important to be specific and factual. Then you will need to affirm them by demonstrating your concern for them, but also let them know that a negative attitude does not allow for the team's best performance. Ask them if they agree that their attitude was out of line, and in the process of discussing this, ask them to repeat the company mission statement and the core values of the team and the business.

Now it's time to create a growth and development plan for this person's attitude. Ask them what attitudes they feel will allow the best chance for their performance and the team's performance to fulfill the mission and the core values of the business. Point out they already have these attitudes, because you've seen them in action. Now get specific and co-create the growth plan with the actions the individual can take to create a contagious positive attitude in themselves.

10. Effort. Many times a lack of performance boils down to simply not doing what's necessary to achieve the goal. If you are dealing with a team member who isn't doing the work, has a lack of hustle, or is inconsistent with their work output, then it is important to identify what the best results mean to them. It's essential to have this in place before disruption, challenge, and change occur, because when they do come, there is no question that hard work and hustle will be part of the essential formula to overcoming them. Looking for the best starts with articulating what the person desires in regard to their job. Do they want to be considered outstanding, average, or below average? Most of the time you will reach an agreement that they want to be considered an outstanding team member. Affirm and agree with them that this is what you want as well. Now ask them how they see their future and what their goals and aspirations are. This could be growth within your organization or a dream to start their own business or go into another field, depending on their position. Whatever their answer is, it's okay to ask them if being a top performer in their current role helps or hurts them in reaching their goals and dreams. (Of course, a top performer in any field has more options.) Now ask them what activities, how often, and how many times these activities need to be done in order to reach top performer status. Be specific in co-creating the growth and development plan around the daily, weekly, and monthly activities they will need to do to consistently achieve the highest level of performance.

Looking for the best means that you know what the best has to do in order to be the best. Many times lack of performance is simply a misunderstanding or lack of knowledge around what it takes to become a top performer and the activities necessary to reach that goal. Coach Leaders understand that it takes time and experience and often regular coaching conversations around effort and activity levels for people to grasp what they need to do to maximize their performance. Coach Leaders not only look for the best in their people, but they also help them identify what the best looks like, and then they celebrate and point out when a team member achieves it. Celebrating the successful completion of activities often comes long before the celebration of the results of those activities. Never forget: results always come *after* effort.

11. Focus on strengths. When challenges come, it's not uncommon for people to become discouraged to the point their output and performance are impacted. As the Coach Leader you can have a powerful impact on performance by focusing on the strengths of each of your people. When work gets bogged down and setbacks occur, it is human nature to focus on what's wrong rather than what's right. Disruption and change often take people away from their strengths, and this can lead to a negative outlook. When someone on your team is in such a situation, it's time to have a private coaching session with them. Their outward attitude may not be visibly negative, but you know their countenance and their output are not what they normally are. This is a good time to ask them how they're doing, what their challenges are, and what their plan is. Once this is explained, you can begin to identify with them their strengths. Sometimes a simple reminder of their strengths is enough to build confidence and get them back on track. In that conversation, ask how you can help them to get a larger percentage of their work in the area of their strengths and perhaps take some load or pressure off in the areas that are not their strengths. Maximum performance often correlates to how much time in the work process is dedicated to the strengths of an individual. Understanding the strengths of your team members requires you to look for the best, and when you do this, you can make sure each person on your team is operating in their strength zone.

12. Humor. One of the best ways to create the right atmosphere is by using humor to lighten the mood. When the grind sets in and discouragement comes because of the challenges and disruption someone is facing, it's always good to reconnect at a human level. Sharing a funny or even embarrassing story about yourself will break the ice and create connection. Don't miss any opportunity for good, wholesome humor. Remember that humor should never be at someone's expense. A good laugh goes a long way in getting people to refocus with the right attitude. I remember being in many company meetings where Dad started with jokes and funny stories. Getting people to laugh with each other creates connections and gets them focused on what's next. If you are looking for some great videos to play in a team meeting, I suggest checking out michaeljr.com. Michael Jr.'s specialty is wholesome humor with a purpose, which is perfect for creating a positive atmosphere with your team.

13. Connect them to others. Think about a time in your career when you were frustrated and stuck. Did you get unstuck by doing the same thing over and over again? Of course not. You had to get new outside information that allowed you to change your perspective or do something differently. Looking for the best when your people are struggling means that you are constantly searching for new ideas that will help them to grow through their most difficult challenges. There are several ways you can connect your people to others. The most common ways are to suggest books or programs that are specific to the challenges and needs your people are having. An effective way to do this is to create a go-to list of people who are experts or gifted at helping with specific challenges that your team regularly encounters.

Suppose a single mother on your team is struggling with work-life balance as she raises her family and meets work obligations. Introducing her to someone who had a similar or same experience and managed it successfully is a great way to create hope in your team member, along with a realistic game plan. Far too often, as Coach Leaders we think it's our responsibility to solve every problem faced by our team. The reality, however, is that our responsibility is to connect our team members with other people who are qualified to help them through the disruption and challenge. At Ziglar, we teach that balanced success means you are successful in all seven areas of life: mental, spiritual, physical, family, financial, personal, and career. As a Coach Leader, it is unlikely you are an expert in more than two or three of those areas. Because of this fact, it is great to create a go-to list of materials and people for each of the seven areas that you can connect your team members with.

14. Affirm their uniqueness. Each person on your team is unique. Unfortunately, many times people will blame their lack of success and performance on their uniqueness. Comparison is always dangerous and often leads to a defeatist attitude. This is especially true concerning a person's unique gifts, talents, and personality. As you are working with someone who is struggling, you will likely hear them say, "I wish I were more . . ." (outgoing, detailed, energetic, educated, etc.). In a challenging circumstance, the default for many people is to focus on what they don't have and how others have an advantage. When you are working with someone on your team who is struggling, it is good to affirm their uniqueness. Let them know it is their uniqueness and their perspectives that, when properly applied, create the value they bring to the team. Their uniqueness, combined with intentionally developing their attitude, effort, and skills, will bring a value to the team that no one else has. As the Coach Leader let them know that your role is not to make them like everyone else, but instead to help them become the best version of themselves. Looking for the best in someone means you recognize them as unique human beings and you see a future for them filled with potential based on how they grow and develop as an individual. The best chance for their success is to maximize and grow their unique gifts and talents as they develop their whole person.

As you reflect on this chapter, write down the future that you see so you can create it. Write down the best possible future so you can look for the best!

Coach Leaders are good finders and are always looking to catch their people doing something good. When you look for the best, you actually encourage the best in your people. Studies have shown that if you only point out mistakes, it does nothing to lessen the likelihood of another mistake. But when you point out and praise a positive action or behavior in an appropriate way, it increases the chances of that behavior being repeated. Looking for the good is a powerful way to grow the atmosphere and the culture on your team that equip everyone to serve and support each other. Now ask the following questions:

- How can you look for the best in yourself and commit to intentionally developing the best version of yourself?
- How will looking for the best in your team allow them to perform at a higher level?
- How can looking for the best in the face of disruption, challenge, and change positively influence your leaders?

Facing the future and preparing your team for the future depends on the virtues of self-control, being positive, and looking for the best. The best way to get out of a hole is to not get in one in the first place. Having self-control lets you focus on building ladders to the next level of performance rather than climbing out of a self-inflicted hole. Your positivity is the fuel that allows your people to see what's possible rather than what's not, and by preparing and looking for the best in every situation, there are far more doors of opportunity open for you to lead your team through.

As you reflect on this section of the book, what do you think each of your people would say about *your* self-control, *your* positivity, and *your* look-for-the-best approach if asked in a confidential assessment? What do you want them to say?

Moving from theory to application is about what you do. What can you implement from these three chapters that will result in your team saying what you want them to when asked about you?

SECTION THREE

WHAT NEEDS TO BE DONE *NOW*?

Virtues Focused on Action Points Leaders
Can Do, No Matter What Is Happening

Love is patient and kind; love does not envy or boast;
it is not arrogant or rude. It does not insist on its
own way; it is not irritable or resentful; it does not
rejoice at wrongdoing, but rejoices with the truth.
Love bears all things, believes all things, hopes all
things, endures all things.

Love never ends. . . .

So now faith, hope, and love abide, these three;
but the greatest of these is love.

—1 Corinthians 13:4–8, 13

When disruption comes, the team immediately looks to the leader to see what the leader is going to do. Will the leader freeze up, act like everything is okay, or overreact? A Coach Leader should be prepared in advance and immediately begin to stand firm in the storm. Never giving up on the mission, the Coach Leader becomes the light that shines hope on the team. Love truly does endure all things, and love shows up in full force at the beginning of the storm and guides people all the way through the storm. When disruption comes, here is what you need to do *now*.

CHAPTER 10

VIRTUE 8: BEING THE LIGHT

Theme: Lead through darkness.

Leadership is about standing out and being visible. The darker it is, the more we can shine as leaders.

Coach Leaders shine the light on purpose and make sure the light reaches everyone they lead. Shining the light and being the light take bravery.

I believe one of the first things a leader should do is illuminate the purpose, mission, and *why* of their organization. Being able to personally commit to the company mission and articulate it in a compelling way is essential. When the team knows you are all in, it removes any doubt and allows them to understand your motives. Visibly committing in the light and then becoming the light take bravery, because everyone knows where you say you stand.

Now that you have fully illuminated where you are leading your people, you need to shine the light on how you are going to lead. Jealousy, dysfunction, gossip, division, and stigma all thrive in the dark. When team members don't know what the others on the team are doing, the shadows creep in, and far too often trust is replaced with distrust. One of the best ways to make sure *how* you do something is correct is to identify the things that can drag your team down. Make sure your leadership shines brightly in that area.

Acknowledge disruption, challenge, and change when they come. As the Coach Leader your team needs to know you are fully aware of every obstacle in front of them. Being the light means you are illuminating the challenges they face, making them easier to address. Being the light also means that when times are darkest, you can dim your own light and focus on turning up the lights of others on your team, which ultimately creates more light and fewer shadows.

Following are seven practical ways you can be the light and make sure your leadership shines brightly.

1. No one left behind. This challenge has been around for decades, if not all of business history. People in the "other" category (temporary, new, uneducated, part time, different, working mom, etc.) tend to get left behind when it comes to promotion, development, and opportunity. We are currently seeing a significant shift in our understanding of location, education, and experience. In the past, people who advanced the fastest in an organization were typically office workers at the company headquarters who were easily available for face-to-face interaction with the upper leadership. Often their education and experience or work history were parallel with the leadership's.

Now everything is changing. The hybrid and remote workforce often means the best and brightest of an organization are no longer available for impromptu face-to-face meetings with leadership. Future needs will depend less on work history, education, and experience and more on the ability to be agile, learn quickly, and adapt rapidly to changing market conditions. The old way of making sure the so-called best and brightest get promoted is now extinct.

As a Coach Leader, no one left behind means that you need to decide how you are going to recognize and develop your people. If you choose to ignore your remote top performers, they will soon be working for your competition or starting their own companies. If you focus only on results, then people will fixate on how to make your system better and will completely miss that no matter how much you improve the system, the system may no longer matter because the market has moved on.

Here are two actions you can take to make sure no one gets left behind:

- If you have a hybrid or remote workforce, consider developing the approach and mindset in your business that remote workers are recognized in everyday activity. The best way to do this is to make sure your company mission, vision, and values are aligned with your policies and procedures manual to support remote workers. If it is understood that company meetings, communications, and policies are geared to support remote workers, then everyone working in the company offices will automatically be included. The reverse is not true, however. One surefire way to alienate your best remote workers is to make them feel left out of company communication, culture, and events.
- Make sure your recognition and development plan for your people requires high levels of engagement, growth, and performance.

Being the light means you are responsible for the engagement, growth, and performance of your people. Far too often we get satisfied with performance and accept this in place of relationship and growth. As the Coach Leader, never forget that people thrive when they are growing and learning in both their professional skills and relationships.

2. Be transparent. Trust is the by-product of integrity, and transparency is the currency of trust. Is it possible to have a good relationship, personal or professional, without trust? Of course not. Integrity creates trust. Transparency allows trust to do its good work. If you don't trust the bank, you'll keep your money under your mattress. If you trust the bank, you keep your money there, and it generates interest and funds new projects. This is the way transparency works with your people.

Being the light by being transparent allows you to create an atmosphere that permits your team to be transparent. When you admit a mistake, seek clarification because you don't understand something, or acknowledge that you don't have the answer, this gives your people permission to do the same thing. Leadership expert Patrick Lencioni has written extensively about how vulnerability is a huge factor in how leaders create successful teams. Oftentimes transparency and vulnerability go hand in hand. It takes courage to shine the light on your own vulnerabilities, and yet this light allows your people to share theirs as well. Long-term growth requires the ability to identify readily and visibly what we don't know and need to learn. Hiding what we don't know makes for a dim future!

3. Let others shine. Coach Leaders understand the best way to achieve business goals is to help their people achieve their goals. This is done through collaboration, co-creation, encouraging, supporting, developing, and equipping their people so they shine.

Plan the shine! One of the best ways to make sure your people shine is to plan it in advance. When you are working with someone on your team, get clarity from the start on what success looks like, and then let them know how you plan on recognizing them when success occurs. Follow through on this and then do a little bit extra. A personal note, an email copied to another leader in your business, a simple team celebration: all these things magnify the light you bring.

4. Make light part of your agenda. Just as hate cannot defeat hate, only love can; darkness cannot defeat darkness, only light can. Because of this, light must be part of your agenda. Lack of clarity or being cloudy on an issue or objective is a form of darkness. As the Coach Leader, it is foundational and essential that you bring light and clarity to the goals and projects of your team. Here are a few key questions to ask:

- What is the desired outcome of this project?
- How will this outcome support our mission and vision?
- What is the deliverable for the project and the due date?
- Who owns the project?
- Does everyone have clarity and ownership of their roles in the project?

Of course, these questions are tactical, and if you're like me, you have seen your share of questions that sound good but are never actually asked. This is why you need to think of "Being the Light" as an empowering, difference-making virtue. Your Coach Leader mindset should take this simple approach: What questions can I ask that will illuminate the challenges we face so we can focus on the solution? Being curious and asking questions with this mindset save time and money!

Here are three more "Be the Light" questions I learned from my mentor Bob Tiede. These are great questions to ask in shorter, often unscheduled conversations:

- How is your progress on your priority from last week?
- What is your biggest challenge this week?
- How can I help?

5. Practice the STICKY method. The STICKY method is a powerful way to get your team to brainstorm so everyone is engaged and involved in the process. Far too often brainstorming and problem-solving sessions simply deteriorate into a discussion between a small portion of the team, the outspoken members. Because there is no intentional focus on clarifying the problem, it is not uncommon that the solutions presented are either incomplete or don't address the core issue. Plus, if only a few people on the team participate, there is a strong possibility the best solutions were never offered. Use the following STICKY method to gain clarity and complete team engagement:

> **S: Say the problem.** The owner of the problem needs to explain it in detail and is free to use a flip chart, whiteboard, or a PowerPoint. Get clarity!
>
> **T: Talk it out.** Everyone in the group asks the owner of the problem clarifying questions. It's very important that no solutions are offered at this stage. Just more shining a light on the problem. Now, rewrite the problem based on this new information.
>
> **I: Invent solutions.** Have everyone in the group write down at least three possible solutions to the problem on sticky notes, one solution per sticky note. No one speaks out at this time. In this way everyone participates and the unlikely genius answer is more likely to appear. If you are doing this via a Zoom call or something similar, have everyone write their solutions in the chat, but tell them not to send the chat with all their answers until you say to do so. In this way everyone is focused on offering their own solutions rather than seeing what anyone else is saying.
>
> **C: Communicate solutions.** Have each person individually read their solutions from their sticky notes or from their unsent chat and explain when necessary. When they are done, they pass the sticky notes to the owner of the problem or send the chat. It is powerful to put these sticky notes on a whiteboard or

flip chart with the identified problem or to copy them into a shared document the team can view on the Zoom call.

K: Know your plan. Prioritize the action steps and create the plan to solve the problem.

Y: You get to work! Determine a timetable and accountability.

6. You shine brightest when your load is the lightest. In the book *Choose to Win*, I use the metaphor of a hot-air balloon as the transportation device to take you to your goals and dreams destination. The basket of your balloon is labeled Desire and is filled with all your desires, goals, dreams, skills, and experiences. On the balloon itself is the word *Hope*, signifying your belief that achieving your desires will give your life meaning and purpose. The furnace of the balloon is where the fuel is burned; the heat comes from that and fills and lifts the balloon. The furnace is labeled Grit, because to get to your destination, to achieve your goals and dreams, it takes a lot of grit! In order to achieve the things in life you want, you have to have a burning desire, a hope that you can do it and it will be worth it, and the grit to keep on doing what you need to do, even when it gets tough. But you also need a knife! Now imagine you are in your balloon as you read the following excerpt from *Choose to Win*.

> Your balloon is really struggling to gain altitude as the white-hot flame of Grit is going full-strength but you are no longer rising! What could be holding you down? You gather up your courage and look over the side of your balloon and you see it. Your balloon is tied to the ground by several ropes! There is one more thing you have to do with your balloon in order for you to reach your full potential. You have to cut the ropes that are holding the balloon down. This takes more Grit! I call these ropes bad habits or the results of bad habits. These ropes include things like the bad habit of limiting

beliefs, or bad health habits, or bad self-talk habits—really any habit that prevents you from maximizing the gifts and talents that God has given you. You grab the razor-sharp knife of wisdom, and with a lot of Grit, you start cutting the ropes of bad habits and limiting beliefs.

As you cut the first rope, you notice it is labeled Limiting Belief. As you cut the rope you say out loud, "I can do this—what others have told me in the past is wrong. I am designed for accomplishment, engineered for success, and endowed with the seeds of greatness." When the rope is cut, the balloon jumps with altitude. You rise rapidly and then it happens again. *Bam!* You look over the side, and another rope is holding you back. This one is labeled Bad Habit. As you cut this one, you start to smile as you gain altitude. Why are you smiling? Simple. You see a lot more ropes, but you have a really sharp knife and a lot of grit. You are now choosing to win! Your balloon is now gaining the altitude necessary to reach your goals and dreams!

As the Coach Leader you must understand that sometimes you are your own disruption and the challenge you have is you. What bad habits do you need to cut out of your life that are holding you down and keeping your light from shining brightly and broadly?

7. Being the light is a responsibility, not a right. Your responsibility is to illuminate what is right. Don't get confused by thinking that, just because you are the leader, you are entitled to have the team follow you. Leadership is not an entitlement but rather a relationship to be earned. When you think of leaders throughout history and in your own experience who had to deal with massive challenges, how many of them failed because they saw their position of being the light as a right rather than a responsibility?

Being the light people want to follow means that you have to own your responsibility for making sure your light is burning brightly, especially in the most difficult circumstances. As soon as you justify making exceptions and compromises that benefit you personally at the expense of those you serve and lead, you abdicate your responsibilities and give your team permission to abdicate theirs as well.

Disruption, challenge, and change are part of life and part of leadership. When darkness comes, it is essential that we understand and take responsibility for being the light that guides our people through the storms. Take a moment to review the seven practical ways you can be the light and make sure your leadership shines brightly. Write the word *yes* beside each of the seven practical ways that applies to you. Now read the following questions and consider your answers, using the seven practical ways that you marked yes as your guide:

- How will I lead myself to better be the light?
- How can I be the light more effectively to my team?
- How can I help my leader's light shine more brightly?

One final thought: being the light is about motive and action. I received the following note from Ziglar Legacy coach Richelle Hoekstra-Anderson. A few months into the pandemic, we recorded an uplifting and encouraging video to help people struggling with the lockdowns. Richelle has a huge heart to help those who are struggling, so she created a five-day Facebook challenge to help. She wrote:

Oh one more thing . . .

I don't know if you know this, but after you and I recorded the Stronger video in the spring, I launched my first-ever five-day FB challenge called Stronger Mindset. For five days I posted a video on rising to the challenge of uncertainty by practicing key resiliency-building tools. It started with sixty people (who signed up when I offered to send them our video if they provided me with their email address) and quickly reached over eight hundred people by the fifth day. The group continues to grow, and I am now up to almost twelve hundred members from all over the world in this private FB group.

It was from this group that I was able to launch the Choose to Win group coaching program. I am just wrapping up my second successful group program and plan to run another one soon.

So I'm Choosing to Win . . . and your inspiration, along with the opportunity to record that video with you, is what caused me to *grow*.

Here is the point: Richelle's motive was to help people, and then she took action. This combination of motive and action allowed her to be the light to more than a thousand people in this one example. And you can do the same!

CHAPTER 11

VIRTUE 9: NEVER GIVING UP

Theme: Be patient and forbearing.

We must set our minds to persevere, to believe that every trial makes us stronger and that every challenge is an opportunity, never giving up, but always focusing on solutions, processes, and progress. In the midst of a crisis, sometimes the best thing to do is nothing. And this takes incredible patience.

> "Muddy water is best cleared by leaving it alone."
>
> —*Alan Watts*

Being patient is the rock you can rest on when everything is being stirred up around you. Being patient is not retreating or giving up, it is simply withstanding the urge to react when there is uncertainty and lack of clarity. Persevering in the storm a little longer rather than running for cover will often allow the time needed to clear the air and see the best course of action.

> Consider it all joy, my brothers and sisters, when you encounter various trials, knowing that the testing of your faith produces endurance. (James 1:2–3 NASB)

As a seventh grader I chose James 1:2–3 to be my life verses. Now, when I look back at this, I wonder what I was going through at that time to pick those verses. From almost every perspective, my life was about as perfect as it could be. Loving parents, good health, and a great school, along with Dad's success in the business world, meant I faced very few real trials. Now, with an additional forty-four years of experience, I can honestly say those verses have made a huge impact in my life, simply because of the way I view trials, perseverance, and endurance.

Saying "never give up" is much easier than actually never giving up. As you read through this chapter, put a plus sign (+) by each section you believe will help you when you are facing a storm with perseverance so you will be better able to never give up.

Consider It All Joy

As a Coach Leader, I challenge you to consider it all joy when the challenge, disruption, and change come. Everything about a challenge should be relished, because with the right mindset and determination, it will make you stronger in every area of your life. When we stress our muscles with weights, the challenge tears down the muscle, but then it is restored and grows back stronger. As we progress in our business career, the challenges we overcome allow us to grow and give us the opportunity and competency to handle more responsibility. The next time a problem shows up in your professional life, either through a business circumstance or a unique relationship challenge from one of your team members, consider it all joy because this test and how you *grow* through it will make you stronger. The consider-it-all-joy attitude and mindset toward the challenge will greatly increase the likelihood of your handling it correctly and quickly.

The Choose to Win Attitude

In the book *Choose to Win* I boldly state on the front cover that you can transform your life one simple choice at a time. We all have a choice—even the choice not to choose—and I believe choosing to persevere, to endure, to be patient is essential to your long-term success as a Coach Leader. Go ahead and choose in advance the attitudes you are going to choose when disruption and challenge come. The mentors in my life have asked me what I would do when challenges come. This simple question does two things. First, it acknowledges that there are always challenges coming. Second, it allows you to better handle the challenges when they show up. The best preparation of all is to create the mindset and muscles before you need them: choose the right attitudes.

Learn from Others Who Have Persevered

History is filled with countless stories of people who overcame incredible challenges in their lives. Reading the stories of Holocaust survivors and those who have survived shipwrecks and other tragedies helps you to understand the amazing potential we all have within us to survive and persevere if we will set our minds to it and focus

173

on the task at hand. Stories from people you know about their lives and perseverance have an even greater impact. I vividly remember the stories Dad told about growing up during the Great Depression, about having to work from the time he was six years old, about going into the sales world and having zero success for the first two and a half years, and about his perseverance. Taking one more step toward his goal allowed him the opportunity for the conversation with P. C. Merrell that changed his life forever. Many times the breakthrough in success only comes after you have put yourself in a position to succeed while standing on the pile of your failures.

Revisit Your Why

When you are faced with a setback, failure, or massive disruption, it's always a good thing to revisit your *why*. I asked my friend Jose Garcia-Aponte what he would do when life knocked him down. His quick response was, "I take a run on the beach and revisit my *why*." What is your *why*? What is your purpose? Is it your family? Your legacy? Something you need to prove to yourself? Is it your faith? Getting clear on why you're doing what you're doing and how success benefits your *why* will allow you to persevere during the toughest storms. Knowing your *why* also has the benefit of keeping you from wasting time and energy on things that do not support and lead to the accomplishment of your *why*.

Call Your *Who*, Mentor, or Coach

My "*who friend*" Bob Beaudine wrote a book titled *The Power of Who*.[11] He described what a *who friend* is, namely, a true friend:

someone you can share your heart with, who holds you accountable, who will do anything for you, and whom you will do anything for. A true friend knows your *why*, your dreams, and the things that keep you up at night. As Bob said, "A true friend knows you so well that, when you forget the song of your heart, they will sing the words back to you." When the trial comes, there is no better person to call than your *who friend*. Never giving up means that we have people we can count on who will stand beside us. Do you have three or more *who friends* in your life? If not, I suggest you devour Bob's book and learn how you can find and grow *who friends*. *Who friends* make all the difference and give you the hope and the encouragement you need to never give up.

A mentor is another great place to turn when you are going through a difficult challenge. Mentors can be great sounding boards, and they typically have relevant experience that can help to guide you through difficult and trying times. Thinking about your mentor's example and even their life story of how they never gave up in a similar situation is a powerful way to stay focused on completing the project before you. Perhaps what's most important is they can encourage you when what you are working on is not getting results. You will likely hear their version of that same or similar experience followed by the encouraging words, "Keep at it! You're getting closer!" Never giving up often depends on following the footsteps of the mentors who have gone before us.

I am sure you will not be surprised when I tell you that you need a coach. Coaches are different from mentors in that they are more focused on helping you to discover solutions than they are in offering solutions. A good coach will remind you of your *why* and ask you questions to help you to find your best path forward. Coaches also understand the power of accountability, and at the end of the conversation will usually wrap it up with some form of this question: "What are you willing to commit to getting done regarding this challenge before our next session?" Accountability is never more important than in the big things of life where giving up is not an option.

Begin Each Day with the Never Give Up Perfect Start

The most powerful habit in my life is what I call the "perfect start." When you choose this habit, every area of your life will improve. The perfect start is simply how you start each day, and the goal is simple: to make your life happen to your day rather than let the day happen to your life. How you start each day is essential, especially when you are fighting dragons in a situation where giving up is not an option. I intentionally invest the first part of every day to building myself up, planning the day, and accomplishing my top priorities. When you are faced with a major disruption or change, this becomes your top priority of focus. Before I lay out the key activities of the perfect start, I want you to keep a few things in mind.

It doesn't matter whether or not you are a morning person. Your perfect start can be tailored to your needs, and it can be short. The key is to get your mind working and thinking intentionally on what you need to accomplish before you start your work for the day.

Start small. I invest ninety minutes or longer in my perfect start, but I didn't begin that way. Ten minutes, even five minutes as you learn this new habit is fine. The key is to do it every day until it becomes a habit. I would rather you do ten minutes a day every day for sixty-six days than do thirty minutes only three or four times a week. The perfect start is a muscle you build. Don't try to run a marathon on your first time out.

Remove distractions. I do my perfect start first thing every morning. I get up, make the coffee, and begin. I don't check email, text messages, social media, the news, or anything else until I've completed my perfect start. The goal is to get your mindset right first, then plan the day, then tackle your objectives for the day.

Create the time. Do the perfect start first thing. Create the time by getting up a little earlier if need be. It is amazing how getting up fifteen minutes earlier and using those fifteen minutes in the perfect start pays you back all day long.

The Never-Give-Up Perfect Start

1. **Five minutes:** Start with gratitude, prayer, and a time of reflection. Settle your mind.
2. **Ten minutes:** Read or listen to something inspirational and life building. This could be Scripture or a book or a devotional. Get your mind thinking in the right direction.
3. **Two minutes:** Review your *why*. Read it to yourself. Confirm it in your mind.
4. **Five minutes:** Journal your thoughts and feelings around the challenge you are facing. Get clarity on the challenge. Focus your mind.
5. **Ten minutes:** Write out the answers to these five questions:
   - What problem do you need to solve?
   - What challenges do you face in solving the problem?
   - What skills and knowledge do you need to solve the problem?
   - Who can help you solve the problem?
   - What is the plan to solve the problem?

6. **Forty-five minutes:** Intensely work on solving the problem with specific actions you can do that day.

Repeat these six steps every day until the problem is solved. Note: You may only need to review Step 5 as the rest may not change much from day to today.

Step Back and Try Something Else

Albert Einstein allegedly said that insanity is doing the same thing over and over and expecting a different result. We have all been there. It is easy to get locked into working harder and harder and doing the same things with more intensity when trying to overcome a problem as you live out the idea of never giving up. Take a step back and elevate your thinking. Reflect on what the problem is and what you have been doing to address the problem. Are you getting traction? Have others done the same thing and gotten results?

Let these questions sit in your mind. Now identify the things you haven't tried and the people you haven't spoken to about the situation. Do some research on the problem at hand. Create a new list of things you could try, and review this several times during the day. Before you go to sleep, review the list and ask yourself: *Which of these should I focus my attention on tomorrow?* Now get a good night's sleep and anticipate a perfect start in the morning with the goal of taking action on one or two new ideas. Many times the new idea will combine with something that has been tried in the past, and the combination will move you toward the solution. Remember, never giving up is not about insanity; it is about persevering and trying new things when you discover what things don't work.

Create Some Momentum by Getting
Wins in Other Areas of Your Life

As a Coach Leader, the primary focus of this chapter is that you demonstrate the never-give-up approach in your pursuit of achieving the mission of your business. When the disruption comes, don't limit your thinking to 100 percent focus on only the problem at hand. If you do, this will drain your energy because of neglecting the other areas of your life. Look at the seven areas of your life—mental, spiritual, physical, family, financial, personal, and career—and pick two or three that need some attention that could boost your overall energy if you had a quick win in those areas.

For example, you realize you're mentally drained and haven't had any good creative inputs and your physical exercise has been suffering because of the time you've invested in work to overcome the disruption. Set a short-term goal for one or two weeks and commit to working out intensely four or five times a week while listening to a personal development program or audiobook that motivates and inspires your creativity. Think of something you enjoy doing that could be a reward for completing this short-term goal. It could be as simple as your favorite meal, but whatever it is, make sure it's something you really enjoy. Getting focused and getting wins in the other areas of your life will often stimulate the creativity and the ideas you need to tackle the problem at hand. One of the hallmarks of top performers in all industries is that they take care to intentionally create energy in the most important areas of their lives.

When you are coaching someone on your team who is in the middle of a challenge, make sure to ask them how they are doing in all areas of their life. Quality of life equaling quality of work is never more important than when dealing with a major disruption, and it is essential for perseverance. Never giving up is fueled by the constant attention we pay to our mental, spiritual, physical, family, financial, and personal lives—not just our careers. When you have a coaching conversation with a top performer who is suddenly struggling with a challenge, you will often discover the root of the issue is a disruption in their personal life. People with problems at home bring those problems to work, and if you can help your team members get some wins in their personal lives, this will help them in their professional lives.

Plan in Advance How You Will Handle the Setback

Those who persevere in times of challenge and change are those who understand that disruption is always coming and who plan in advance how they are going to handle it. Most people will plan in advance for the physical challenges that come. This most often can be seen in savings accounts and cash reserves. Mature Coach Leaders do this by constantly training and developing their people to learn new skills, preparing them for the future, and fostering a growth mindset. The most important way to prepare in advance is also the most overlooked: preparing your attitude and mindset.

When the going gets tough and the days grow long and weary, it's easy to fall into the trap of a negative mindset. If you're not careful, your tone and your self-talk will turn into a constant and droning whining. "Why me?" "When is this going to end?" "What if we don't fix this?" "How bad can it get?" "Just great, more bad news!" Have you ever been there in your own thinking? Most of us have. Now ask yourself, *Does any of this thinking and self-talk help me to overcome the problem, to persevere, to never give up?* That is an easy question to answer.

As a Coach Leader, you need to train your mind in advance. When the challenges and setbacks continue to pile up, automatically begin to say these things:

- Another opportunity to learn!
- What is this teaching me?
- Fantastic!
- Solving this problem will be epic!
- I am grateful I have my team to address this challenge!

Let's identify what we can control and do something about it.

The US Marines have a fantastic approach to creating the never-give-up mindset before they go into battle. They are trained to *improvise, adapt,* and *overcome* any obstacle in whatever situation they find themselves. Marines relish the challenge, and if you hang around a marine when they are facing a serious setback or challenge, you will hear them say under their breath these three great words: *improvise, adapt,* and *overcome.*

Understand the Power of Incrementalism

Baby steps. Almost everyone overestimates what they can do in a short time and underestimates what they can do over a long time. Persevering through a major challenge is always accompanied by hundreds of baby steps that incrementally add up to a major victory. Just as in the previous section regarding the perfect start and making sure to take care of all areas of your life, it is important to break down your challenge into the different areas you can control. You cannot control whether your customer says yes, but you can control the presentation you give and the research you do.

Use incrementalism to break down the problem into separate parts and focus on improving each part by 1 percent. Perhaps you are working with a salesperson on your team. They have been struggling and you are convinced they can make it if they will never give up. Break down your sales process into the key parts:

- Mindset
- Quality of leads
- Number of outbound calls
- Introductory conversations
- Discovery calls
- Formal presentations
- Asking for the business
- Overcoming objections
- Getting referrals
- Getting testimonials

Depending on your selling environment, there may be more or fewer components to your sales process than what's listed here, but the principle is the same. Look at each category and, with the person you are coaching, ask them how they can improve each by 1 percent this week. As you can see, the 1 percent improvement covers every area of their role, their attitude, their effort, and their skill. Never give up! By an inch, it's a cinch!

Refocus on the Foundation

Once it becomes clear that you are faced with a major disruption or challenge, then it is wise to review and refocus on the foundation on which your business is built. By this time in the process you should have already reconfirmed and clarified your *why*. Now is the time to refocus on the foundation that your *why* and your business are built on. What is the problem you can solve? What is the solution you can offer? What is unique, better, and different about your solution or service? What are the principles and values you live by as you solve the problems of your customers? Are you satisfied with the foundation you see? If not, you need to get to work on the foundation or it is likely any short-term gains you start to see because of increased energy and effort will be temporary. Remember, when the storm comes, it often reveals the stability of the foundation on which your business is built.

Elevate Your View of the Situation

As you continue to persevere and overcome major business challenges while you are working with and developing the people on your team, make sure that you take time to elevate your view of the situation. Look at your business or the challenge from the view of a customer or the market or from views of other people on the team. What has changed? Is business being done dramatically differently? Has a new technology disrupted your industry? Are people making different decisions now than they did in the past? Is it likely that things will go back to the way they were? By elevating your view of your challenge, you get clarity on what has changed. Never giving up also means that we embrace what has changed.

Dump the Old Plan

One of the interesting conundrums in times of rapid change and disruption is that organizations that have a thoroughly thought-out five-year plan (or longer) and are loyal to the plan are the ones most likely to suffer. When the COVID-19 pandemic changed how and where millions of people worked, it didn't change the need to serve and solve the problems of their customers. The old system for face-to-face team meetings and strategy sessions suddenly was no longer possible. As a Coach Leader, never giving up means you are constantly searching for a new plan that will take you where you want to go. The quicker you let go of a plan that no longer works, the faster you can embrace a new plan that has a chance of working.

The Story You Tell Yourself

The most powerful story in the world is the story you tell yourself because it determines your thinking, your thinking determines your performance, and your performance determines your results. What is the story you tell yourself when you are surrounded by challenges and disruption? Are you grateful? Overwhelmed? Humbled? Excited? Steadfast? As you lead your team and yourself, do you think, *Why would they listen to me?* Instead you could think, *I am here for a reason and I'm ready to be part of the solution.*

I heard about a First Nations group in Australia who were often called in to do rain dances in times of drought. They had a 100 percent success rate. One of the group elders was asked how it is that they had such a tremendous success rate, and the elder responded, "Simple. We dance until it rains." This is the ultimate never-give-up approach, and clearly the story you tell yourself will determine how long you're willing to dance.

Every No Is One Step Closer to Yes

Never giving up means that you look at the nos and the failures as simply steps that are taking you one step closer to the answer. When I was in sales, I kept a daily tally of how many people said no to my offers.

Whenever I received a no, I would smile because I knew I was one step closer to a yes. Why did I smile? I had tracked for months how many nos it took to get a yes, and I knew that for every seven nos I would get a yes. Focus on what you can do and focus on how you do it and embrace the fact that not every effort will get the result you want, but it will help you to learn and gather information on how to solve the problem.

Don't Be a SNIOP

SNIOP is a term Dad coined many years ago. It stands for Susceptible to the Negative Influence of Other People. SNIOPs have little chance of leading their people through difficult times. Negativity is something none of us have to look for, because it simply shows up, especially when we don't need it. Coach Leaders are constantly on the lookout for people who encourage and lift them up and are very protective rather than on the lookout for anyone who would negatively influence their mindset or their team's morale. Make it a point, as you discuss options and plans to overcome a challenge with your team, to evaluate the communications you are receiving in terms of its being positive or negative. If someone who has the team's ear or has positional authority is negative in their communication style, make sure you address this with your team so you can limit the negative impact it will have. As the Coach Leader, it is a given that if you are a SNIOP, your team likely will also develop a negative attitude and morale.

You Are Setting the Example

Whenever I'm flying to a destination and we encounter bad weather, I always keep an eye on the flight crew. If the crew continues to operate professionally and doesn't exhibit any visible stress, alarm, or concern, then I know everything is okay. I trust they have all the best information, and based on that, they are making good decisions. As Coach Leaders, our body language, our tone of voice, and our words either comfort our team or raise concern. What messages are you sending?

There are so many things that can help you persevere and never give up in the midst of challenges, and all of it is added up and bundled into the example you set. Your people will do what you do and react or respond in the way you react or respond. Being confident about your course of action, even when you haven't discovered the answer, is critical in leading your team. Because of this, you must set the rhythm of preparation and growth from day one.

Set the Rhythm from Day One

Knowing and planning for disruption means that you understand the day is coming when you will have to live out the never-give-up approach. This means that from day one, starting with recruiting, onboarding, training, and development, you must plan to create a rhythm of learning, growing, and relishing the challenges that come.

As you move into the future, recruiting top performers will be an extremely important and competitive area you must be concerned with. Top performers can work for almost any company from anywhere. Their market value is higher than ever before, and their ability to pick and choose where they want to work has never been more in their favor. In the recruiting process you need to be clear about the mission of your business, the values you hold and operate by, and especially your view on how you will address disruption and change. As you recruit top performers, they need to know your view on how you will address the problems that come. When they see your confidence and even excitement for the changes that are coming, they will know they are in the right place.

Onboarding is an essential step in confirming that your new recruit is a great fit. In the onboarding process make it clear that you believe there is no such thing as one-and-done training. This means that training and growth are constant. You will actively participate and make sure these are aligned with the company mission, and you understand both the personal and professional goals of your people so you can help develop them toward success in every area of their lives. As you onboard people, let them know that you will always take time to learn what's essential to know for future success, even when facing crises and deadlines in the present.

Training and development are not only essential for professional advancement in business skills, but they are also essential for life skills. In order to build a team that will adapt, overcome, and improvise regardless of circumstances, your team will need to be rock solid in every area of their lives. Quality of life equaling quality of work is perhaps the most important foundation to perseverance and never giving up. A team that is doing well both personally and professionally has the reserves to go the extra mile when the battles come. The first casualties when times are tough are those who were already suffering in other areas of life, such as their physical health or their relationships at home.

When quality of life issues are neglected, this impacts the mindset of the team and limits the capacity of your team members to perform under pressure and in times of disruption and change. As their Coach Leader you must make sure from day one that everyone on your team understands the importance of mindset, growth, training, and development both professionally and personally. You demonstrate this by example, and when the day comes and it's time to display the never-give-up approach, your team will be with you to walk through the trial side by side. Together, you will emerge stronger and better able to solve the problems of those you serve because of it.

Ultimately, never giving up is an intentional choice every Coach Leader has to make. Change, challenge, and disruption are coming. When you know and believe in your *why* and your purpose and your role as the Coach Leader, and you have alignment with your company's mission, vision, and values, then never giving up becomes more than a slogan; it becomes your heartbeat softly echoing in your ears when the disruption comes.

Reflect on the following questions:

- How can I set an example through my attitude and commitment in personal and professional growth so the never-give-up approach becomes automatic when challenges come?
- How can I prepare my team now in every area of their lives so they are optimally positioned to excel when disruption and challenges come?
- How can I support and prepare my leadership for change and disruption in advance of the situation?

CHAPTER 12

VIRTUE 10: STANDING FIRM

Theme: Be worthy of trust in tough times.

During tough times we need the posture of a strong spine and an open heart. Leading with integrity is like a lighthouse in the middle of a hurricane.

> "Trust is the by-product of integrity."
>
> *—Tom Ziglar*

My wife and I had the opportunity to see the musical *The Greatest Showman* with Hugh Jackman in the starring role. The movie version is my favorite movie of all time. It strikes a powerful chord with me because it is a metaphor for what we do at Ziglar. We help people to understand and believe they are worthy of dignity with gifts, talents, and character qualities that they simply need to recognize, claim, develop, and use. Every quality of success is already inside us, but we must develop them.

The Greatest Showman is about P. T. Barnum and how he put

together the Greatest Show on Earth by featuring the misfits of society. The bearded lady, the giant, the fat man, the tattooed woman, little people, the list goes on and on. The movie emphasized and recognized the greatness inside each of them and gave them a stage on which to shine even though the world rejected them as different and unworthy. In the movie, Barnum transferred his confidence to all of them, and this helped them to grow into outstanding performers.

The trust that Barnum earned from his team was because of the trials and attacks he endured on their behalf. In the movie, his people were ridiculed and called freaks. Barnum defended them, stood by them, and when invited by the Queen of England for an audience, agreed to go only if all of his team were welcome. Barnum realized his greatness depended on his people's greatness.

The movie's anthem song, "This Is Me," is powerful. The lyrics speak for themselves, and over and over again they affirm that, even with our scars and our differences, we are all glorious. The song makes you realize that no matter how someone looks or acts on the outside, on the inside they are asking themselves the questions: "Am I enough?" "Do I have what it takes?" "Will I get hurt again if I open up?" I encourage you to watch the music video if you want to get a lift in your spirit.[12]

As powerful as the anthem is, the song and the message are set up from the beginning. The opening of the live show that we saw was magical: full-on inspirational and uplifting music and performances that built into an incredible crescendo, ending with Jackman at the very end of the extended stage and in the middle of the audience. His chin was up, his chest thrust out, his spine straight, his arms down, and his hands back. He was 100 percent confident and 100 percent vulnerable. It was as if every ounce of his being was saying, I present to you my team and I am so confident and proud of them that I give you my open heart.

Warrior Spine, Open Heart

When you are able to stand firm like a lighthouse in the middle of a storm, you create an incredible confidence in your team that leads to productivity and performance. The image I have of this is Hugh Jackman at the edge of the stage. His posture was a combination of the warrior spine and the open heart.

The warrior spine is represented by his chin up, back straight, and chest out. Not only was his posture saying *this is me*, but it was also saying *this is us*. We have done it before, we are doing it now, and we will do it again. On top of this, his arms were down and extended, with his hands pulled back. This is the open heart, and it represents that he is all in, vulnerable and transparent, holding nothing back. In this pose you know without a doubt that the Barnum character knows his team: every fear, every weakness, every strength, every hope, and every dream. And you also know the team knows this about him as well.

And that is the key.

During times of disruption, as the Coach Leader, your team needs to see you standing firm in the storm at the front of the business stage. This inspires trust, creates confidence, and boosts performance. It also requires vulnerability—the open heart—because this creates trust. Vulnerability starts with you.

Leadership expert and author Patrick Lencioni observed:

When team members trust one another, when they know that everyone on the team is capable of admitting when they don't have the right answer, and when they're willing to acknowledge when someone else's idea is better than theirs, the fear of conflict and the discomfort it entails is greatly diminished. When there is trust, conflict becomes nothing but the pursuit of truth, an attempt to find the best possible answer. It is not only okay but desirable.

At the heart of vulnerability lies the willingness of people to abandon their pride and their fear, to sacrifice their egos for the collective good of the team. While this can be a little threatening and uncomfortable at first, ultimately it becomes liberating for people who are tired of spending time and energy overthinking their actions and managing interpersonal politics at work.[13]

Trust is created through vulnerability, and it is built on the foundation of integrity.

The lighthouse that survives many hurricanes does so because it is built on solid rock. Integrity is your foundation, and vulnerability is the light through which trust shines brightest.

The Power of Identity: Creating Trust Through the Transparency of Your Story

Never underestimate the power of your personal story. It is your greatest asset. I didn't fully understand this until I read Daniel Coyle's *The Talent Code*.[14] He includes an example of a classroom study in which math students were introduced to a new branch of algebra. The teacher explained that this branch was discovered long ago and gave some brief background on the mathematician who had discovered it. The teacher then explained how to solve problems using the formula. At the end of the class, a test was given about the new information, but there was a twist. In the middle of the test was a brief biography of the mathematician that included his birthday. Half the class was given a version of the test on which the mathematician's birthday matched the students' birthdays. The other half of the class received a version on which the birthdays didn't match. The study filmed the students as they took the test. The students who thought their birthday was the same as the mathematician's worked on the problems 30 percent longer than those whose birthdays didn't match. That's incredible. Because they identified with the mathematician, they worked longer to solve the problems.

When people went to hear Zig Ziglar speak, they thought, *Wow, this Zig guy is really good. He is smart, funny, charismatic, a great speaker. He knows all the rich and cool people. He is good looking, wealthy, etc. I could never be like Zig Ziglar.* Then Dad would tell his story:

I was born in L.A.—lower Alabama—and raised in Yazoo City, Mississippi, during the heart of the Great Depression. I was the tenth of twelve kids. My dad died when I was five, and I was raised by a mom who had only a fifth-grade education. I started working at six years of age, selling peanuts on the street corner, and I have worked ever since. I never did well in school. In fact, I was in the part of the class that made the top half possible! I entered the navy after high school, then went to college and didn't do well or graduate. I got a sales job and didn't sell anything for two and a half years. Well, I did—I sold my furniture, my car. You get the picture. Then one day everything changed.

At this point in Dad's speech, you could almost feel the audience change. People began to think to themselves, *Well if he can, maybe I can.*

This is the power of identity. The mood in the room *had* changed. "If he can, maybe I can." No longer was Zig Ziglar some unknown expert with superpowers, he was just a normal person like everyone else in that room, and he had to overcome enormous challenges, just as everyone else in that room. Not only did people take notes, they also took action. Because they identified with him, they took action 30 percent longer on his recommendations, and that extra 30 percent was enough for them to get a positive result. So they tried the next thing he recommended and the next, until their whole lives had changed. You have this power of identity as well. The people you are trying to influence need to know your story. They need to know it wasn't always easy for you. You have scars, you have overcome great challenges, and you have made some bad decisions along the way. When they see the transparent, real you, they will identify with you. When they identify with you, they will try what you recommend 30 percent longer and get results.

Isn't it amazing that standing firm requires integrity and trust that is best created by being vulnerable and transparent? For you to have performance-impacting influence as a Coach Leader, your team needs to implement the plans you co-create with them. When they identify with you through your stories of not knowing the answers, making mistakes, taking ownership of your mistakes, and getting outside help when necessary, they are far more likely to not only take action and do their part, but they will also seek out help and admit when they are stuck and need help.

Standing firm through the warrior-spine-and-open-heart approach also enables you to better access the years of experience you are already surrounded with and create team ownership of the goals, projects, and plans you have co-created with your team. I love the story below that David Mattson shares in his book *The Sandler Rules for Sales Leaders* about team ownership:

> Let me share the precise moment when I realized this core leadership truth. Years ago, I had a bad habit of taking on too much and trying to solve every problem myself. During one of our coaching sessions, David Sandler (who had dropped hints about this issue several times before) asked me, "How many years of experience in business do you have, Dave?"
>
> Proudly, I said, "Ten."

"And how many years of experience does your team have?"

I did a quick and dirty calculation involving the experience of the twelve people who reported to me, and then said, "240."

He nodded and then stared at the ceiling thoughtfully, as though he were considering an intricate math problem. I knew that when Sandler did this, it meant a lesson of some kind was on the way. He didn't disappoint.

"So are you saying," he asked, "that you would rather solve this problem with ten years of experience than with 240 years of experience?"

I didn't have to answer. The lesson was clear.[15]

As a Coach Leader you must embrace that standing firm means that integrity is your foundation and vulnerability is the light through which your trust shines brightest. When you do this, productivity and performance are increased.

- How can you lead yourself and intentionally stand firm and yet be vulnerable and open?
- What examples can you set that will allow those you lead to engage when vulnerability is required?
- What questions can you ask your leaders in one-on-one meetings that would open up their vulnerability and allow you to be a valuable resource?

CHAPTER 13

CREATING YOUR FUTURE

Disruption is coming faster and faster. What future do you want? Take a moment and imagine you are watching a movie of yourself in the leadership position of your dreams. The chaos of the world doesn't matter, because you are leading from the ten virtues.

Those you lead know:

1. *Kindness* is your automatic response to people regardless of the news.
2. You serve from a position of *selflessness*, knowing that helping others helps you.
3. You start new relationships and affirm old ones by showing *respect* for the person in front of you.
4. You exercise *humility* when you hear ideas and learn new things as your curiosity leads to amazing new insights.
5. You do best when the pressure gets intense because *self-control* is second nature to you. In fact, you have learned that personal attacks handled with self-control elevate your leadership influence over time.

6. You are *positive* because they can feel your positive attitude. They feel better about themselves and the future whenever they communicate with you.
7. You *look for the best* in every person and every situation.
8. You are *the light* in dark times and illuminate with clarity the way ahead.
9. You *never give up* on them, their hopes and dreams, or the mission of the team.
10. You *stand firm* with a warrior spine and an open heart regardless of the disruptions, challenges, and changes around you.

Taken together these ten virtues mean you are leading from a position of love. This love does something powerful: it creates an atmosphere that allows vulnerability to flourish. When you and your team are vulnerable with each other, there is no masking, no excuse making, and no need to hide what you did wrong or what you don't know. Individuals and teams that do the best in times of disruption are the ones who will quickly admit they are stuck, don't understand, or made a mistake. This rapid acknowledgment of the imperfect allows for rapid adjustments and accelerated learning, which advances the team and the mission.

A New Way to Look at Vulnerability

An atmosphere of vulnerability is hard to create in a traditional office environment where everyone is spending so much face time together. As time goes on, more and more work will be done remotely, with people working on teams and projects from different locations and different time zones. This asynchronous work will often be recorded in online document tools such as Slack or Google Docs. If it's hard to be vulnerable face-to-face with the people you spend hours each day with in the same office, imagine how hard it will be to be vulnerable in a written online document that will be viewable forever.

World-Changing Asynchronous Work Will Require Asynchronous Vulnerability

I believe asynchronous vulnerability is the ultimate fruit of the Coach Leader who lives out the ten virtues in every relationship. When everyone on the team is able to be vulnerable, no matter where they work from or what hours of the day they work, something magical happens: trust starts to blossom. Asynchronous vulnerability is simply trust not bound by time or space. Coach Leaders create an atmosphere of trust that allows for teams to work in unison, regardless of where the people on the team are. Simply put: trust not limited by when or where.

Another way to look at this is that asynchronous vulnerability is a fancy word for *faith*.

As a Coach Leader who is living out the ten virtues, your people develop faith in you, in themselves, and in the other members of the team. Isn't it amazing that almost all business crises are really crises of faith? Isn't it even more amazing that the solution to business disruption is really a *soul*-ution! Love makes faith possible, and with love and faith, there is hope in the future.

So now faith, hope, and love abide, these three; but the greatest of these is love. (1 Cor. 13:13)

When the ten virtues are combined with the Coach Leader skills described in this book, you can love your people and leave a legacy.

Legacy: The Ultimate Goal of the Coach Leader

Legacy is teaching and transferring the habits that build character, integrity, and wisdom, which will ripple through eternity. Legacy is far more than passing on knowledge; it is about the everyday application of that knowledge in the form of habits that produce a life well lived.

Legacy is the reputation, character, integrity, and wisdom that are successfully transferred. This concept really hit home when I talked with my friend Clifton Jolley. Not long after my dad passed away, Dr. Jolley asked how I was doing.

I said that Dad's legacy was heavy on my shoulders.

He said, "Tom, your dad's legacy is secure. There is nothing you can do to hurt it. The only legacy you have to worry about is the one you will leave."

Dad equipped me with more than I could have ever hoped for, but my legacy is up to me. As Coach Leaders, our role is to equip our people with everything they need to build their own legacy, along with the ownership to do so.

- Legacy is not money; it's living a life that creates money as a by-product of a life well lived.
- Legacy is about transferring habits that build great relationships with family, friends, coworkers, customers, and God.
- Legacy is preparing those you love to grow through life's most difficult challenges.

As a Coach Leader your ultimate legacy is how you prepare those you lead and love to reach their fullest potential and empower and equip them to leave a legacy of their own that ripples through eternity. Legacy inspires legacy.

A Final Word

"The greatest of these is love."

—1 Corinthians 13:13

As you set your mind to become the best Coach Leader possible, I encourage you to keep it simple as you develop the ten virtues in yourself and implement all the techniques and strategies in the book. The Coach Leader game plan gives you a usable sequence of success you can grow with and equip those you lead to do the same.

And yet if you do all this book contains without love, it will be to no avail. Perhaps another way to look at becoming an outstanding Coach Leader is to consider that only one virtue really matters, and that is love, and all the other virtues are simply ways of expressing love. After all, if you love yourself and those you lead and God, wouldn't you follow though in expressing that love in ways that allow yourself and others to become the people God created you to become?

The Next Level

If you are ready to go to the next level as a life-changing Coach Leader, then I encourage you to dig into the appendices of this book and to visit www.ZiglarCoachLeadership.com to get a bunch of great additional resources and to learn more about our Coach Leadership Training Class and our Coach Leadership Coaching Programs.

ACKNOWLEDGMENTS

I have so many people to thank for helping me with this book! Over the last eighteen months, countless hours have been invested in research and conversations with so many people from all walks of life that have given me insight and inspiration into what Coach Leadership really is.

I want to start by thanking my immediate family—Chachis, Alexandra, and Zach—for listening to my book ideas when they were trapped in the car, at the dinner table, or taking walks with me.

Bruce Barbour, my friend, mentor, agent, and book writing genius, for his countless hours and thousands of nudges on the book.

The entire Thomas Nelson team, with a special thanks to Jenny Baumgartner and Janene MacIvor for asking the great questions and polishing the book with incredible skill. You guys are a joy to work with!

Laurie Magers for your incredible support and editing and to Cindy Ziglar Oates for your constant encouragement along the way.

My Who friend, Bob Beaudine, with whom I could have deep conversations and dream a little at the same time about the book.

Howard Partridge, friend, mentor, and the best small business coach in the world, who made the book so much easier to understand.

Owen Fitzpatrick, who got the whole concept rolling at a breakfast just before the pandemic hit and suggested a few books to read and a path to explore.

John Rouse and David Wright, for their encouragement and lively discussions around everything coaching in a way that pleases God. This book is a reflection of our discussions!

Dr. Rashmi Dixit, for helping me to see how to address the sensitive subjects of Coach Leadership in ways that lift up those who are often disregarded and equip leaders to put aside preconceived notions that limit their effectiveness.

Michael Norton, Trenell Walker, Scott Eriksson, Bryan Dodge, Billy Cox, Bob Tiede, Charles Ho, and Krish Dhanham, who each have sharpened my iron through the years in their own unique way.

Grant Estrade, who is not afraid to call me out for the purpose of discovering and testing the foundation of my thinking, making it stronger and richer in the process.

TJ Johnson, Jason Frenn, and Julie Ziglar Norman, whose voices I hear in my head as I seek to speak the truth in love.

Kevin Miller, who is the greatest podcast host in all the land—for the countless hours we have discussed the issues in life that matter most.

Angie Crellin, who inspires and equips our Ziglar Coaches on a daily basis to become Coach Leaders and has inspired me in the process.

Seth Godin, Rabbi Daniel Lapin, Ken Blanchard, and Dave Ramsey, who are my mentors through the written word and who are always quick to give direction and positive feedback when I ask.

STEP-BY-STEP COACHING PROCESS

"You must *be* the right kind of person and *do* the right things before you can *have* all that life has to offer."

—Zig Ziglar

This quote is especially true for Coach Leaders. Following is a step-by-step coaching process (the *do*) that will allow you to inspire, develop, grow, and lead a top performing team and business. Most of all, as a Coach Leader you will want to inspire your people to *do* this for themselves. The *do* process is designed to be intentional, and it will take some time, but the results are exponential. Doing this effectively with more than five to seven direct reports could be a stretch for you if you have other leadership requirements beyond coaching and developing your people. The *do* process is exponential because your ultimate goal is to develop leaders who can also implement the *do* process.

Step 1: Choose to Be a Coach Leader

Intentionally choosing to be a Coach Leader is the first step you must take. The key here is to avoid being lukewarm. You need to go all in. This means that you need to intentionally develop your mindset, your habits, your character qualities, and specifically the ten virtues and skills necessary so that being a Coach Leader is the automatic fruit of your life. Let this book serve as your guide as you become an incredible Coach Leader.

Step 2: Choose to Do the Coach Leader Game Plan

To be a great Coach Leader you need a game plan. Just as in sports, leading a team in the business world means you will face both expected and unexpected challenges. The game plan you have prepared in advance will have a huge impact on your ability to adjust when the disruption comes.

Ziglar Game Plan Form: Before the Game Begins

The Ziglar Game Plan Form can be found here:

www.ZiglarCoachLeadership.com.

You are welcome to use it or you can create your own based on your organization's needs and priorities. Make sure you complete the form for each of your team members before the game begins.

Company Mission

The company mission statement should be at the top of your game plan form, and you should have it internalized and memorized. As you onboard and work with team members, keep in mind the company mission statement is your true north, and the more you reference it, the more likely you will continually move toward it.

Team Mission

Depending on the size of your organization, you may want to create a team mission statement that describes how your team specifically fulfills the company mission statement. This is especially helpful in organizations that have many tiers and divisions. A team mission statement can better connect a team member's work to the overall success of the business.

Team Members' Job/Role Descriptions and KPI

As the Coach Leader you need to have complete clarity in identifying the job description and role for each of your team members. Identified KPIs (key performance indicators) are essential in this area. As change and disruption come, many job descriptions become outdated and are no longer useful. Reviewing this regularly allows you to adjust as your team members grow and as the work changes.

DISC Profile of Team Members

The DISC profile is a powerful way to understand the communication styles of your team members. Having the DISC Profile Assessment done for everyone on your team will allow you to communicate with each team member in the way they can best receive it. This is more important than ever if you have a remote or hybrid workforce and your communications are done primarily by video conference. You can learn more about the DISC assessment tool and get yours here: www.ZiglarCoachLeadership.com.

Words That Motivate and Connect with Team Members

Make sure to highlight on your game plan form the words that motivate and connect with each team member as revealed in their DISC assessment. Highlight words, phrases, and questions that are specific to each person's DISC profile. It is also a good idea to make note of things you should never say to that team member, based on their profile. This is also a place where you can take notes regarding past conversations with team members, emphasizing what words worked well and what words didn't.

Team Members' Personal Motivators, Dreams, and Goals

This section of the game plan form definitely evolves over time. In the beginning, new team members might be hesitant about sharing their personal dreams and goals. It might be limited to their career goals and may seem limited and small. As you gain trust and the relationship builds, you will begin to understand what their overall personal motivators and goals are. When you learn something new, make sure to add it to the section. This can be a topic for further discussion. For example, if they say they would like to travel, ask them what their dream trip would be. How they answer that question will tell you how much this motivates them and will allow you to help them reach this goal. Remember that goals and dreams take time and money to accomplish. The better someone does at their work, the faster they can attain their goals and dreams. My book *Choose to Win* is a great resource for this section. As a Coach Leader, it will help you to help your people get clarity on their *why*, their dreams, and their goals, and it is based on the powerful growth concept of "the fastest way to success is to replace bad habits with good habits."

Team Members' Attitude

Identify the attitude and character strengths your team member already has, and identify the attitude and character qualities your team member needs to work on to excel in their role. As challenge and disruption come, the strengths or weaknesses of their attitudes will become apparent and will allow you to coach them to develop this area. (For more detail see page 220.)

Team Members' Effort

In the team member's job description you should have clearly identified the specific activities the team member needed to do in order for them to be successful. These are measurable efforts and activities that set the team member up for success. In a sales role, for example, it is common to give a team member a quota. A salesperson's day may consist of different efforts and activities around research, outbound calling, emailing, presentations, and proposals. Tracking these activities on a daily basis will allow you to guide them on the appropriate amount of time to spend on each activity to reach their goal. The team member's effort is focused on how often the activity is done. Make sure each of your team members knows exactly what the expectations are for each activity that is central to their success. (For more detail see page 220.)

Team Members' Skill

The team members' skill is about identifying their competency and professionalism. Do they have the knowledge base and the expertise to do all aspects of their job at the highest level? With disruption and change, if activity levels and effort remain the same but results are going down, the first place to look is in the knowledge and skill level of each team member to determine if they are keeping pace with the changing business world. (For more detail see page 220.)

Step 3: Choose to Do the Coach Leader Coaching Process: Discovery, Strategy, Accountability, and Growth

Now that you have a game plan tailored for each team member, this establishes a benchmark that will allow you to successfully guide and coach each person so they can maximize their performance. When setbacks occur because of personal situations or disruption and challenges in the workplace, having the game plan as a benchmark is an incredibly valuable place to start. In fact, the team member might be doing very well based on the standards you set, but they are highly motivated and want to do even better. Now, with the game plan, you have the ability to compare what was expected, what they did, and then create a new plan for what they want to accomplish. The good news is it doesn't matter if it's a lack of performance or a desire for improved performance, the game plan allows the Coach Leader coaching process to work efficiently and effectively. Here are the steps in the Coach Leader coaching process:

Discovery

In the discovery phase with your team member you should be curious and ask questions about what is going on regarding their performance. You will want to focus on their mindset, attitude, effort, and skill. You will need to do this meeting in private, and you will want to let them know up front that the goal of the meeting is to understand where they are and then create a strategy to get where they want to go. In the discovery phase you will ask such questions as:

- What is your goal for your performance?
- What is holding you back?
- What has changed in your work?

- What do you wish were different?
- What attitudes do successful people in this area have?
- What activities and efforts do you need to increase?
- What knowledge do you need to be more productive?
- What skills do you need to improve on?

Remember, as a Coach Leader your mindset in the discovery phase is to uncover and draw out the more capable person inside your team member.

Strategy

The second phase of the Coach Leader coaching process is strategy. The discovery phase was to establish the mindset and what needed to be done. Strategy is about creating an action plan that can be implemented that will allow the team member to move toward their goal and own the plan they co-create with you. The following are the components necessary to co-create a plan the team member will take ownership of:

Agree on the Challenge. As you begin the strategy phase, start with reaching agreement on the identified challenge that was uncovered in the discovery phase. This challenge needs to be written down and agreed to as the problem to solve in order to move forward.

- *Can you reach clarity on the thinking and feeling of the customer of the team member facing the challenge?*

    No matter what role a person has on your team, they have customers who count on them to help solve their problems. Customer service agents, salespeople, support, supervisors, and every person on the team are responsible for doing the work that helps someone else and fulfills a need they have. Ask the team member what the customer is thinking or feeling in regard to the problem or solution and what the team member can do to help resolve it. Ask your team member what problems the customer will face if the problem is not solved in a professional way. When your team member is clear on how the customer is impacted and how the customer thinking and feeling about life because of the problem, it helps the team member to understand why the combination of solving the problem with the right attitude, effort, and skill is so important.

In the HVAC example given in appendix C, the team member identified the homeowner with the broken air conditioning system was experiencing uncomfortable heat inside the house and was very concerned about the cost to fix the problem and if he could trust the technician who was there to solve the problem. When a team member gets clarity and anticipates how a customer is being impacted by a problem, it allows them to prepare in advance how to ease those feelings to best solve the problem.

Another example involved a vice president of sales I once worked with. The VP was challenged with serving three different customers at the same time, all with different expectations. The first two customers were his internal customers—his legal team and his marketing team. His job was to deliver a keynote that included a lot of technical information and required strict legal guidelines. The marketing team created a PowerPoint presentation for him to use, filled with technical jargon and legalese that resulted in a boring presentation. The third customer was the audience of his presentation, which consisted of existing clients and future prospects. The presentation's goal was to develop stronger business relationships with audience members by booking appointments with them.

I played the Coach Leader role and asked the VP how his customers (his legal team, the marketing team, and the people for whom the presentation had been prepared) were feeling before he began the presentation and how he wanted them to feel when he was done. He said that legal and marketing were concerned about accuracy and that the audience was likely already tired and bored before his presentation even began. He told me he wanted to satisfy his internal customers and create excitement in the audience to book appointments following the presentation. As a result, he created a shorter PowerPoint with interesting slides that made it easy for him to tell stories, and he kept the technical slides for the Q&A session. In this way he met the goal of setting appointments and was also prepared to correctly answer any questions, making legal and marketing very happy.

Now, based on your team member's feedback and your knowledge and experience, write out in detail what the customer is dealing with concerning the problem and how this is impacting their thinking and feeling.

- *What do you want the customer to think, feel, and do when the problem is resolved?*

Now ask your team member to imagine that they have completed the work perfectly. The customer is absolutely satisfied, they are feeling and thinking very positively about the experience, and their trust is so high they would gladly give a testimonial and a referral regarding the work done by the team member.

We create the future we see, and the future we want to create in this case is a completely happy and satisfied customer. List out in detail all the thinking, feelings, and results the customer will have when they experience a phenomenal job by the team member.

- *What attitudes are necessary to move the customer to the desired outcome?*

Ask your team members to identify the attitudes they will need to engage with the customer in order to take them from their initial thinking, feeling, and discomfort, before the problem was solved, to the desired outcome you want. Make a detailed list of the attitudes the team member comes up with. Now co-create an action plan with your team members on how they can grow and develop these identified attitudes.

- *What effort is necessary to move the customer to the desired outcome?*

Ask your team member the effort, activities, and hustle they will need to demonstrate in order to change their customer's thinking, feelings, and discomfort from what it was before they addressed the problem to what you want their thinking/feeling to be after the problem is solved. Make a list of observable physical actions the customer can witness that will create the desired outcome. Examples could include being five minutes early, being organized, moving with purpose, and even leaving the place cleaner and doing a little bit extra. Now create an action plan with your team member on how they can intentionally and purposefully demonstrate these visible actions.

- *What skills are necessary to move the customer to the desired outcome?*

Ask your team member to think about what skills they need to improve in the professional and relational areas of their job role. Does your team member need more training in order to be more effective in their job? Go over the job description with your team member and identify together the skills needed to do their job with excellence. Ask your team member how they rate themselves in each skill area and if they believe improving in these areas will get them better results. Now co-create an action plan with your team member on the skills they are going to develop in order to improve their performance. Remember, skills are not limited to technical skills but also include essential relationship skills.

Accountability

Once you have co-created the strategy with your team member, set up an accountability structure that allows you, as the Coach Leader, to check in and inspect what you expect. A great way to roll this out is to confirm a follow-up meeting that gives your team member a reasonable amount of time to take action. Depending on the challenge the team member has, this could be as short as the next day, but generally it is about one week. The timing of the follow-up meeting will depend on their specific job role and their ability to implement the improvements they are working on. A simple question at the end of this meeting to gain accountability would simply be, "What daily actions are you willing to commit to before we meet again?" Let your team members commit in their own words, because this will create ownership and will reveal how much they are buying into the plan they co-created with you.

The accountability process also allows for check-in conversations along the way. These can be stand-up five-minute hallway conversations or Zoom meetings as you check in on each person on your team. Two questions that work very well for a check-in are "How are you coming along on the plan we created together?" and "What can I do to help you with the plan?" The point of accountability check-ins is to make sure your team member knows you are focused on their needs, and when you have your scheduled meeting to discuss progress, nothing should be a surprise to you.

Growth

As the Coach Leader your primary focus and mindset for each of your team members when they are facing challenges, change, and disruption should be about their growth. Job performance is a given and is always important, and this is what most organizations measure, and rightly so. As the Coach Leader, however, you can never focus on results at the exclusion of growth. Organizations that do this eventually go out of business when disruption comes, because they keep doing what no longer works. For this reason, your primary objective is to help each of your team members grow in a way that, when they face new challenges and disruptions, they are empowered, because they have learned to coach themselves through the process you have taken them through.

Team members who are aware of their own strengths and weaknesses, who know how to address these on their own, are the ones who thrive in times of disruption. By implementing this coaching process with your team members, you are equipping them to be Coach Leaders of themselves and others! This is incredibly important in the new remote and hybrid workforce. Mastering a new attitude, effort, or skill is essential to performance. Teaching your team members how to identify on their own what they need to develop in themselves is the difference between being average performers and top performers.

Step 4: Choose to Inspire, Influence, Impart, Introduce

As a Coach Leader in the *be, do,* and *have* process, you will have to intentionally choose who you are, how you come across, and how you motivate others.

Inspire

Everyone on your team and in your organization, as well as those you serve, needs hope and encouragement. As a Coach Leader your greatest contribution is exponential growth. How can you exponentially multiply your impact? Inspiration is the key! To inspire means to breathe life into another person. Part of your daily habit should be to identify at least one way you can inspire either an individual or the entire team as they go about their work and their life. "How am I going to inspire my people today?" is a great question to reflect on as you start your day.

Influence

As John Maxwell observed, "Leadership is influence, nothing more and nothing less." As a Coach Leader, sometimes it can be faster and easier to just solve the problem and tell people what to do. But the ultimate goal is growth in your people, and because of this, it is far better to ask questions that help your people discover the solution. As a Coach Leader your goal is to guide and shape the right mindset. Remember, the number-one limiting factor of your influence is the example you set.

Impart

As you develop your team there will be many opportunities to impart ideas, concepts, systems, knowledge, and wisdom that you have learned and studied and used throughout your life and career. The idea of imparting means you are encouraging those on your team to voluntarily embrace what you bring to them rather than dumping it on them or mandating it. Imparting comes with a moral implication, and the ten virtues should be the base of motivation through which you share new information. One of the biggest things you can impart or transfer to your team members is confidence. Many times your belief that your people can do more than they think they can will actually lead them to do more than they think they can!

Introduce

As the Coach Leader you should always be looking for opportunities to introduce your team members to ideas and concepts that will help them grow to the next level. When introducing a new idea or concept, ask for permission, especially when a person is frustrated or stuck with the results they have been getting. When permission has been given, ask them what they have been doing that is not working. As you dig deeper into this, you will often discover that bad habits are the limiting factor in your team member's performance. One of the most powerful things you can introduce at this point is the idea of replacing the bad habit with a good habit. Ask your team member, "What would happen if you stopped doing [the bad habit] and started doing [the good habit]?"

Step 5: Choose to Have a Top Performing Team

When you choose to *do* the previous four steps, then you have chosen to *have* a top-performing team. Having a top-performing team gives you many options. You are able to give and grow in ways that are impossible when your team is not performing. Can you give something you don't have? Of course not. What is the ultimate gift you can give? I believe the ultimate gift is *legacy*.

Appendix B

COACHING WORKSHEET

A downloadable Coaching Worksheet is available on our resource page at www.ZiglarCoachLeadership.com.

Name: [name of the team member]

Job Description: [Put their complete job description here.]

DISC Profile: [List their personality profile here with the list of tendencies found in the DISC assessment. You can use other profile assessments if you are already using them.]

Words That Inspire and Connect with This Person: [From the DISC, list the words that connect and communicate with the person.]

Personal Motivators, Dreams, and Goals: [List everything the person has shared with you about goals, dreams, and aspirations (to get a promotion, pay off debt, buy a car, travel, etc.). This allows you to connect what they do (their job) with achieving their goals and dreams.]

Skill Training Focus for the Week: [List the training you are currently doing with this person so they can put what they learn into action.]

Weekly Game Plan

Attitude: [List the attitudes your team member identified as important to their success (see appendix C). Ideally, you will want your team member to write out how they are going to work on these attitudes and why this is important to get the results they want. Use the team member's description rather than your own, because this creates ownership.]

Attitude Focus for the Week: [For example, "I know you are working on several areas of attitude. Which one are you going to focus on this week and how can I help?"]

Effort: [Activities required this week to hit weekly goals (for example, calls, emails, appointments, proposals, projects, deliverables, preappointment planning and preparation). This list should be co-created with your team member, and ideally all or most of it should come from your team member. If something you believe to be important is not on the list, ask questions to help your team member discover this rather than just tell them.]

Question You Will Ask to Discuss Weekly Expectations: [For example, "Which action is your top priority this week and how can I help you to be successful in this?"]

Skill: [What specific skill is the team member working on this week? List the skills your team member said they wanted to improve in order to get the results they want. As the Coach Leader you are focused on helping your team member grow, so it may be appropriate to ask questions not only about the skills they need to flourish in their current role, but also questions about the skills they need to develop to advance in their career.]

Questions You Will Ask to Discuss This Skill Development: [For example, "What skill that you have listed, if you could have mastered it this week, do you think would give you the greatest results? How can I help you to develop that skill?"]

Mental Model: [Before you have a coaching conversation with your team member, review the Coaching Worksheet that you filled out from prior meetings and take a minute to do a mental model. During this minute imagine how you want the conversation to go and what questions your team member may have. Reflect on what is working well for your team member and any areas they may be struggling with. Are their relationships positive with other team members, leadership, and customers? Are they doing well at home? Are they making progress toward their personal goals? Is their attitude, effort, and skill on track and growing? What questions can you ask them to increase their ownership and action toward their goals?]

EXAMPLE OF A COACHING CONVERSATION

Coach: Hi, John. Thank you for meeting with me. I appreciate all that you are doing during these challenging times. I am grateful for your contribution and want you to know you are making a difference. How are you doing?

John: Doing fine. These are interesting times, aren't they?

Coach: Yes, they are. Your family doing okay? I know having the kids home from school has to be a big change.

John: We are adjusting. Some of it has been tough, but compared to so many others, we are doing pretty well.

Coach: That's good. The reason I wanted to meet with you is I have been thinking about our business and our plans for next year, and I wanted to get your input and some ideas from you as it relates to your own goals. I see a lot of opportunity for you and our business, and I want to make sure we are on the right track. Is it okay if I ask you a question?

John: Sure, go ahead.

Coach: As we come to a close for this year, I want to ask if you want to make more money next year, the same money next year, or less money next year?

John: Is that a trick question? Of course I want to make more money next year.

Coach (with a smile): Yes, I suppose that is an easy question. The good news is I want to pay you more money. And of course, to do that, the business has to be doing well, and you have to be a reason the business is doing well. I thought it would be good to talk about a plan for you that would allow you to earn more money next year. Does that sound fair?

John: Paying me more money always sounds fair to me! What do you want me to do?

Coach: Before we get into the what and how, can you tell me why you want to earn more money? Is there something specific or special that earning more money would allow you to do?

John: Mainly just bills to pay off and some credit card debt. More money would be a big help on that.

Coach: Once you've got that taken care of, is there anything else you would use the money for?

John: Well, my wife and I would really like to save up for a down payment for a new home and get out of renting.

Coach: That is fantastic! Do you guys already have something in mind or is this something that you have just recently started discussing?

John: We have been talking about it for some time now, but it just seems so out of reach because of the uncertainty.

Coach: I get that. I remember how I felt when we bought our first home. It can be pretty scary. Is there anything other than the money that is holding you back on getting your home?

John: Mainly just the money. But I really have no clue how the process works and how much house we can afford and where to even get a loan or a real estate agent we can trust. I guess I just have lots of questions that aren't worth asking until the money comes together.

Coach: That's the way I thought as well, and then a good friend shared something with me that changed my thinking and allowed me to get a house several years sooner than I thought possible. He told me to write down exactly what I wanted in my dream house and then put in place a plan to get that dream house. He gave me Zig Ziglar's Performance Planner to use and actually helped me to flesh out what I needed to do. I realized I needed a budget and a lot of education on how buying a house works. But the biggest change for me was my dream house was so clearly defined in my mind and my plan was so rock solid that it allowed me to resist impulse purchases and short-term decisions that would delay getting the house. Before I knew it, we were moving into that house! Would you like me to get you a Performance Planner? I would love to help you in any way I can.

John: Yes, that would mean a lot to me.

Coach: Consider it done! Now I would like for us to develop a plan around your job that makes sense to you so you can earn more money. I really like the Ziglar Performance Formula described in *Choose to Win*. It simply says that attitude times effort times skill equals performance. In other words, our attitude with our customers and each other impacts our performance, as does our effort and hustle, as does our skill level and professionalism. These three multiplied together either build or break a business. We have to be good at all three, because if any of them is bad, we will lose customers and stop getting referrals. Does this make sense, John?

John: Yes, I think so. Could you maybe explain how it works with attitude so I can get a better understanding? I think I have a good attitude, so I am not sure where you are going with this.

Coach: Absolutely. And you do have a good attitude. I am just thinking if we approach it from a different perspective, we can create a *wow* attitude with our customers and with each other. Our attitude is the way we come across to others, and it includes our words, our expressions, our tone, our eagerness, and our presence. I have another question for you. When you show up at a home and the AC is broken and the inside of the house is a sweatbox, what do you think the homeowner is thinking and feeling when you start to talk to them?

John: That's easy. I deal with this every day. They are wondering how long it will take to get it fixed, and they are worried about how much it is going to cost them, and they are very concerned if they can trust me.

Coach: Tell me more.

John: They are also wondering if I will do a good job and fix it right, and if it's a woman, she is often concerned for her family's safety, since they don't know me. Sometimes I feel as if they are comparing me to the last service person who was in their home, and usually that's not good, because they have been burned before.

Coach: Perfect. I think you hit all the major feelings and thoughts our typical customer has in that situation. Since you understand how the customer is feeling when you show up, what attitudes from you do you think would put the customer at ease and help you get a five-star review?

John: I think it starts the moment I get there. Since I know their worry and concern levels are high, my attitude and demeanor need to be polite, upbeat, courteous, and confident. Anything I can do to put them at ease, build trust, and let them know I am a professional is going to be essential.

Coach: So what attitudes do you think are the most important for you to display?

John: I have never thought of it this way. . . . I am thinking empathy, confidence, being present, hopeful, encouraging, trustworthy, and professional.

Coach: Fantastic. Now, how can you prepare and develop those attitudes before you ring the customer's doorbell?

John: I am not sure what you are asking.

Coach: How can you be intentional in making sure you come across with empathy, confidence, being present, hopefulness, encouragement, trustworthiness, and professionalism?

John: Ahh, I get it. I guess it starts the night before. Making sure I get plenty of sleep so I can prepare in the morning without feeling rushed. If I review the service call notes before I arrive and I get there early, they will know I am focused on them. I can make sure the truck is clean and fully stocked, so the service call has the best chance of being completed on a single trip.

Coach: Good. What else?

John: I know you are always listening to inspirational and educational programs as you drive around, so I can do the same thing to make sure my attitude of encouragement and hope is fully fueled.

Coach: Good. What can you do to create confidence, trustworthiness, and show professionalism through your attitude?

John: In my initial conversation with the customer, I can thank them for trusting us enough to call us. I can affirm their decision by letting them know how long we have been in business and that our goal is always to deliver a phenomenal customer experience that would make it easy for them to give us a five-star review and refer us to their friends. I can then show them the checklist and how we diagnose the problem, how we will keep them informed, ask them questions about what is going on, and then present them with our findings and possible solutions.

Coach: Fantastic! You really get how attitude sets the tone for putting a customer at ease and is the first step in creating a raving fan. Why don't you take a minute and write down the actions you are going to take to create the attitude we just discussed?

John: Okay. . . . I have them written down. What do you think? [Presents list of actions.]

Coach: Perfect. Exactly what you came up with and what we discussed. Now let's talk about the second part of the Ziglar Performance Formula. Effort. As you remember, the formula is attitude times effort times skill equals performance. How do you plan on demonstrating effort to the customer that will result in them being happy and giving us a five-star review and referrals?

John: I think demonstrating effort is about all the little things we can do. It's about being on time. Taking care to be clean, like putting booties over our shoes. Leaving an area cleaner than when we found it. Moving quickly and with purpose but not coming across as rushed. Keeping them informed on our progress takes a little extra effort. Even following up with them after we leave to make sure everything exceeded their expectations would be a nice touch and would require some extra effort.

Coach: It sounds like you have the effort part down pat. Our customers regularly comment on how you go the extra mile. Would you write down under effort the things you are going to do? I plan on sharing these with the rest of the team!

John: Here you go! Is this what you were wanting?

[Presents list of actions.]

Coach: Yes. Exactly what I was looking for and a great effort plan. Now let's talk about the third part of the formula. Skill. What skills could you demonstrate to the customer that would build their confidence in us as a service provider?

John: This is where I think I need some help. I consider myself pretty good as a technician, since I have been doing this for several years. But there are a few systems I am not that comfortable with that I come across from time to time. They take more time to fix than they should, and sometimes I have to call you for help. I know this creates uncertainty for the customer and unneeded stress. I need some additional training on these systems.

Coach: Let me know what HVAC systems you need help with, and I will get you scheduled for some training. Also, next time you have a call with one of those systems, let me know, and I will go with you and do some training while we work on it. What else on the skill side?

John: Well, to be honest, I am uncomfortable when it comes to sharing with the homeowner what problems we have found and what our recommended solutions are. As you know, most of the time we find several things that need to be fixed, and the cheapest solution is not always the best solution, since it will often mean we will have to return and fix the unit again and the previous money was wasted. I don't want to come across as high pressure, but I want to present with confidence the best way to go.

Coach: John, that is definitely the right motive. What is best for the customer. How would you want to be treated if you were the homeowner in this situation? Would you want to be shown only the cheapest option or only the best option?

John: I would want to understand all the options, and then, based on the condition of my air conditioning unit, which solution would give me the most value. I would want the expert to recommend the best option for me and still give me choices.

Coach: Yes! So what skills do you need to develop to give our customer this experience?

John: I need to get really comfortable and confident with sharing options with the customer that educate them, letting them know what I recommend, and finally giving them the choice of what they want to do and what that likely means for them.

Coach: Excellent! That sounds really good and somewhat familiar.

John (with a smile): Yes, it does. Just like you have been teaching us for a long time now. Why does it seem like such a good idea now when before it seemed like a mechanical script?

Coach: Could it be that you are starting to understand the sales and service process is not something you do *to* someone but something you do *for* someone? Our customers call us because they have a problem, and our job is to help them out of the problem and do whatever we can to help them avoid future problems and to do all of this with the highest degree of integrity and your best attitude, effort, and skill. Now, write down what you are going to do to develop these skills in yourself. I want to see what you come up with.

John: Here you go. Let me know what you think.

[Presents action list.]

Coach: What you have written down here is perfect. Your plan to develop your attitude, effort, and skill is right on the money. Do you believe if you implement this plan you will get more referrals and five-star reviews?

John: Yes, I do. I like it because it covers all the things I can control.

Coach: What would it mean to you if you got more referrals and five-star reviews?

John: Hopefully this would help our business grow and I would get bonus money for being a key part of that growth. Plus, as I increase my skills, I become more valuable to the business, which is good for both of us. (Sly smile.)

Coach: Why is increasing your value to the business, improving your skills, and earning more money important to you?

John: Because, if I do this, my job security goes up and I get closer to owning my own home.

Coach: I agree completely. Now you are working for your dream and not just a paycheck. That is a powerful motivator. One last question.

John: Sure.

Coach: Is it okay if I hold you accountable to the plan you created?

John: Yes. Absolutely.

Coach: Great! I know you are going to have your best year ever. I am going to schedule a short check-in meeting with you each week, either right before or right after our regular team meetings, so I can make sure I am giving you the support you need and to make sure your plan is working great. Does that sound good to you?

John: Yes!

DISC PERSONALITY ANALYSIS

A Powerful Way to Understand People
Using the DISC Personality Concept

Each Person Has Unique Personality Traits
DR. ROBERT ROHM

Each person's perspective is built into who they are. Some people call it "personality," and some refer to it as "temperament."

Ever notice how different your family, friends, and coworkers can be from you? If you are like me, you have asked yourself, *Why did they do that?* or *What were they thinking?* The starting point of understanding people is to realize and accept one simple fact: everyone is not like you!

Have you ever said the same thing to two people and received two totally different reactions? How can saying the same words produce such different results? Each person "heard" you differently based on his or her personality style. You said the same thing, but what they "heard" was different.

Different is not bad, it is just different. A lack of understanding ourselves and others can lead to real problems such as tension, disappointment, hurt feelings, unmet expectations, and poor communication. As you know, it is hard to work with a problem, especially if you do not understand what is going on inside the mind of another person.

There Is a Simple Way to Understand People

At the Zig Ziglar corporation, we believe the DISC Model of Human Behavior helps you understand how people behave and what motivates them. This concept will allow you to unlock the mystery behind developing good people skills and creating better relationships. It can help to reduce conflict, improve productivity, and relate with others more effectively.

Some Background on the DISC Model of Human Behavior

Twenty-four hundred years ago, scientists and philosophers, most notably Hippocrates, began to recognize and categorize differences in behavior that seemed to follow a pattern.

Since then, many psychologists and scientists have explored behavioral patterns. Dr. William Marston wrote *Emotions of Normal People* in 1928 after earning his doctorate from Harvard University. Marston theorized that people are motivated by four intrinsic drives that direct behavioral patterns. He used four descriptive characteristics for behavioral tendencies which are represented by four letters of the alphabet: D, I, S, and C. Thus the concept of "DISC" was introduced.

Building on a Wellness Model

Many behavioral models focus on what is wrong with a person to identify personality disorders. The DISC model is based on normal behavior, not abnormal behavior. DISC is a wellness model that is objective and descriptive rather than subjective and judgmental. Therefore, DISC is a practical way to understand yourself and those around you in the common settings of everyday life.

A Positive Approach

The DISC wellness model is a good framework for understanding people. DISC should be used in a positive way to encourage a person to be his or her best—not as a way to label someone.

Healthy, positive relationships come from having an accurate understanding of yourself and others. DISC is a powerful tool for obtaining a new appreciation for our personality styles and their effect on our everyday lives.

We apply the DISC model with four main ideas that allow it to be used appropriately as an effective and encouraging tool:

- We use a positive approach to highlight and encourage a person in his or her strengths.
- We use a positive approach to address a person's possible blind spots without assuming a weakness exists.
- We recognize that each person has a unique blend of all the major personality traits to a greater or lesser extent.
- We recognize that behavioral patterns are fluid and dynamic as a person adapts to his or her environment.

I have a saying that "your strengths should carry you while your blind spots should concern you." Being able to identify and articulate your strengths can be very empowering. Being able to identify and uncover blind spots can also be very empowering. The next few pages can be the start of your own empowering discovery process.

So, now that you know where the DISC concept came from and the importance of having a positive, flexible approach, let's take a look at the Model of Human Behavior using the DISC.

The DISC Model of Human Behavior is based on two foundational observations about how people normally behave:

Observation 1: Some people are more outgoing, while others are more reserved. You can think of this trait as each person's internal motor or pace. Some people always seem ready to go and dive in quickly. They engage their motor quickly. Others tend to engage their motor more slowly or more cautiously.

Observation 2: Some people are more task-oriented, while others are more people-oriented. You can think of this as each person's external focus or priority that guides them. Some people are focused on getting things done (tasks); others are more tuned in to the people around them and their feelings.

With both observations, we want to emphasize that these behavioral tendencies are neither right or wrong or good or bad. They are just different. We are simply identifying normal behavior styles. People have different styles, and that is okay.

Four Major Personality Traits

In review, we have four behavioral tendencies to help us characterize people:

- Outgoing
- Reserved
- Task-oriented
- People-oriented

Everyone has some of all four of these tendencies at different times and in different situations. However, most people typically have one or two of these tendencies that seem to fit them well in their everyday behavior. And, on the other hand, one or two of these tendencies usually do not fit them well, and these tendencies may even seem "foreign" to their approach to life. The balance of these four tendencies shapes the way each person sees life and those around them. By combining the two previous diagrams, we can show four basic quadrants of the circle as shown below. Thus, four basic personality traits emerge from our diagram corresponding to the four quadrants of the circle (in clockwise order):

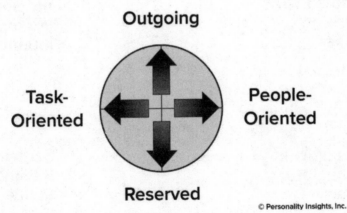

© Personality Insights, Inc.

Diagram 1

- Outgoing and task-oriented (upper left quadrant)
- Outgoing and people-oriented (upper right quadrant)
- Reserved and people-oriented (lower right quadrant)
- Reserved and task-oriented (lower left quadrant)

Get Your Unique Assessment Here

Next, we will add descriptive terms for each of the four main personality types that emerge in the diagram. The descriptive terms will begin with D, I, S, and C.

Describing Each Personality Style

There are four different personality types with four different priorities. Notice the letters D, I, S, and C appear in the four quadrants of the circle in the figure below. You will also notice that descriptive terms have been added in each of the four corners of the diagram. Now we can further describe each of the four main personality styles:

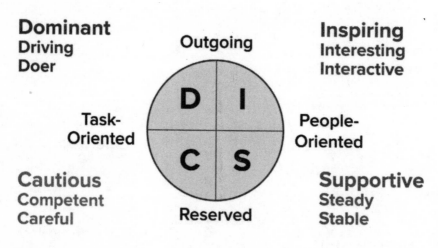

Dominant
Driving
Doer

Outgoing

Inspiring
Interesting
Interactive

Task-
Oriented

D | I

C | S

People-
Oriented

Cautious
Competent
Careful

Reserved

Supportive
Steady
Stable

Diagram 2

D-I-S-C Descriptive Terms

1. **The Dominant "D" type.** An outgoing, task-oriented individual will be focused on getting things done, accomplishing tasks, getting to the bottom line as quickly as possible and "making it happen"! The key insight in developing a relationship with this type of person is respect and results.

2. **The Inspiring "I" type.** An outgoing, people-oriented individual loves to interact, socialize, and have fun. This person is focused on what others may think of him or her. The key insight in developing a relationship with this type of person is admiration and recognition.

3. **The Supportive "S" type.** A reserved, people-oriented individual will enjoy relationships, helping or supporting other people, and working together as a team. The key insight in developing a relationship with this person is friendliness and sincere appreciation.

4. **The Cautious "C" type.** A reserved, task-oriented individual will seek value, consistency, and quality information. This person focuses on being correct and accurate. The key insight in developing a relationship with this individual is trust and integrity.

NOTES

1. Many of these ideas of the future come from Scott Halloway, *Post Corona: From Crisis to Opportunity* (New York: Portfolio/Penguin, 2020) and Peter H. Diamandis and Steven Kotler, *The Future Is Faster than You Think* (New York: Simon & Schuster, 2020). The most striking thing I learned is this: these trends, good and bad, have been accelerated by ten years because of the pandemic. These include telemedicine, remote working, and online shopping. But the rate of acceptance and adoption is mind-blowing.
2. Charles Duhigg, "What Google Learned from Its Quest to Build the Perfect Team," *New York Times*, February 6, 2016, https://www .nytimes.com/2016/02/28/magazine/what-google-learned-from-its -quest-to-build-the-perfect-team.html.
3. For more information about the DISC Personality Profile, see www .ZiglarCoachLeaderhip.com.
4. Jennifer Robison, "The Emotional State of Remote Workers: It's Complicated," Gallup, December 15, 2020, https://www.gallup.com /workplace/327569/emotional-state-remote-workers-complicated.aspx.
5. Duhigg, "What Google Learned from Its Quest to Build the Perfect Team," *New York Times*, February 6, 2016.
6. Diamandis and Kotler, *The Future Is Faster than You Think.*
7. Steven Fry, *True Freedom: What Christian Submission and Authority Look Like* (Grand Rapids, MI: Chosen Books, 2008).
8. Quoted in Dom Nicastro, "Does Netflix CEO's 'Pure Negative' Comment on Working from Home Have Merit?" Reworked, October 22, 2020, https://www.reworked.co/digital-workplace/does-netflix -ceos-pure-negative-comment-on-working-from-home-have-merit/.

9. Angela Duckworth, *Grit: The Power of Passion and Perseverance* (New York: Scribner, 2016).

10. Daniel Coyle, *The Talent Code: Greatness Isn't Born. It's Grown. Here's How.* (New York: Bantam Books, 2009).

11. Bob Beaudine, *The Power of Who: You Already Know Everyone You Need to Know* (New York: Center Street, 2009).

12. See *The Greatest Showman*, "This Is Me," with Keala Settle, 20th Century Fox, https://www.youtube.com/watch?v=XLFEvHWD_NE; *The Greatest Showman*, "This Is Me" (Official Lyric Video), https://www.youtube.com/watch?v=Rj4Yu9Utdw0)

13. Patrick Lencioni, *The Advantage: Why Organizational Health Trumps Everything Else in Business* (San Francisco: Jossey-Bass, 2012).

14. Daniel Coyle, *The Talent Code: Greatness Isn't Born. It's Grown. Here's How.* (New York: Bantam Books, 2009).

15. David Mattson, *The Sandler Rules for Sales Leaders* (Annandale, NJ: New Legacy Books, 2017).

About the Author

Tom Ziglar is the proud son of Zig Ziglar and the CEO of Ziglar, Inc. He joined the Zig Ziglar Corporation in 1987 and climbed from working in the warehouse, to sales, to management, and then on to leadership. Today, he speaks around the world; hosts *The Ziglar Show*, one of the top-ranked business podcasts; and carries on the Ziglar philosophy: "You can have everything in life you want if you will just help enough other people get what they want." He and his wife, Chachis, have one daughter and reside in Plano, Texas.